IPAD FOR SENIORS & BEGINNERS

The Illustrated Step-By-Step Guide Book, A Comprehensive Manual for the Non-Tech-Savvy to Explore the Rich Features of iPadOS with Confidence

By Archer FOX

Table of Contents

Chapter 1: Introduction

1.1 Welcome to the World of iPads

- A brief overview of what iPads are and how they have revolutionized personal technology.

iPads are like magical, slim books that can do almost anything you'd wish for in today's world. Made by Apple, a company known for its innovative products, iPads are a type of tablet computer – a flat, portable device that's much lighter and more convenient than a traditional computer.

What makes iPads so special? They have a touch screen, meaning you can operate them simply by tapping or swiping your fingers on the screen. This is much easier than using a mouse or keyboard, especially for those who might find small buttons challenging.

These devices can help you stay connected with your family and friends, watch your favorite shows, read books, play games, and even attend virtual doctor's appointments. iPads come with a built-in camera, allowing you to take photos or video call your loved ones.

iPads have truly revolutionized personal technology by making it more accessible and user-friendly, especially for seniors. They've opened up a world where staying informed, entertained, and in touch is easier than ever, all from a device that fits comfortably in your hands.

In the upcoming sections, we'll explore more about different iPad models and how you can choose the best one for you. Get ready to embark on an exciting journey into the digital world with your iPad!

- Discuss the ease of use and accessibility features that make iPads ideal for seniors and beginners.

iPads are a true testament to the idea that technology can be both powerful and easy to use, making them ideal for seniors and beginners. Let's explore why iPads are so user-friendly and how their accessibility features open up a world of possibilities.

1. **Intuitive Touch Screen Interface:** The touch screen of an iPad is what sets it apart. It eliminates the need for a mouse or keyboard. You interact directly with what's on the screen, which is more natural and straightforward.
Zooming in or out on photos, web pages, or documents is as simple as pinching your fingers together or spreading them apart. This gesture-based control makes navigating through the iPad's features a breeze.

2. **Simple and Clear Layout:** The iPad's interface is designed to be clear and uncluttered. Icons are large and labeled, making it easy to find what you're looking for, like the email app, camera, or your favorite game.
The home screen is customizable, allowing you to organize your most-used apps and features front and center, reducing confusion and saving time.

3. **VoiceOver:** VoiceOver is a groundbreaking accessibility feature for those who have difficulty seeing. It's a screen-reader that tells you what's happening on your iPad using spoken descriptions.
With VoiceOver, you can navigate your iPad even if you can't see the screen. It reads out text, buttons, and even provides descriptions of images and emojis.

4. **Siri:** Your Personal Assistant: Siri is like having a helpful assistant at your side. You can ask Siri to send messages, set reminders, or even ask for the weather forecast—all with your voice.

For seniors who find typing difficult, Siri can be a game-changer. It's also a friendly companion, always ready to answer questions or help with tasks.

5. **Magnifier and Larger Text:** If small text is a challenge, the iPad has you covered. You can easily enlarge the text on your screen, making reading more comfortable.

The Magnifier feature turns your iPad into a digital magnifying glass, which can be very handy for reading small print in books, newspapers, or even menus.

6. **Hearing Aid Compatibility and Visual Alerts:** iPads are compatible with a range of hearing aids, ensuring clear audio for those with hearing impairments.

For those who are hard of hearing, visual alerts can replace sound alerts. The iPad can flash or display a visual cue for notifications, so you never miss an important message or reminder.

7. **A World of Apps:** The App Store on your iPad is like a treasure chest. It has millions of apps, many of which are designed specifically for seniors and beginners. Whether it's for health monitoring, learning new skills, or just for fun, there's an app for almost everything.

8. **Long Battery Life:** iPads are known for their long battery life. You can use them for hours without worrying about recharging. This means you can read, play, learn, and explore throughout the day on a single charge

- Testimonials or quotes from seniors who have incorporated iPads into their daily lives.

1.2 Differences Between iPad Models

- Detailed comparison of current iPad models (e.g., iPad, iPad Air, iPad Mini, iPad Pro).

As you venture further into the world of iPads, it's important to understand the different models available. Each iPad has its unique features, and choosing the right one depends on what you want to use it for. Let's take a closer look at the current models to help you make an informed decision.

Our journey begins with a clear understanding of the evolution in iPad design, dividing them into two distinct categories. On one side, we have iPads that retain the classic, time-honored design featuring the Home button, symbolizing ease and familiarity. On the other side, we explore the modernized, sleeker iPads that have embraced a new era of technology by adopting gesture-based navigation, offering a more seamless and immersive user experience.

Older iPads: Button Control

Home Button: Older iPads prominently feature a physical "Home" button below the screen. This button serves as the central control for many actions. A single press takes you back to the home screen from any app, double-pressing shows recently used apps, and holding it down activates Siri, Apple's voice assistant.

Control Accessibility: The tactile feedback of the Home button makes it easy to use without looking, beneficial for those not as comfortable with touch screen technology. It offers a straightforward, consistent way to navigate the iPad.

Simplicity and Familiarity: The physical button provides a sense of familiarity, especially for those transitioning from traditional computers or phones with buttons. It's simple, direct, and leaves little room for confusion.

Newer iPads: Gesture-Based Navigation

Removing the Home Button: In newer iPad models Apple has eliminated the Home button. This change allows for a larger screen size and a sleeker design.

Intuitive Gestures: Navigation is now based on gestures - movements you make on the screen with your fingers. For example, swiping up from the bottom of the screen takes you to the home screen, and swiping up and holding brings up recent apps.

Learning Curve: While gestures provide a more immersive and modern experience, they can take some getting used to, especially if you're accustomed to the Home button. However, once mastered, gestures can be more efficient and intuitive.

Accessibility Features: Despite the removal of the Home button, Apple has ensured that accessibility is not compromised. Features like AssistiveTouch allow users to perform gestures more easily, and VoiceOver supports those who need auditory assistance.

As we navigate through this chapter, we will thoroughly review each iPad model currently available on Apple's website. This exploration is not just about listing features and specifications; it's about understanding what each model brings to the table and how it fits into the diverse spectrum of user needs and preferences.

1. iPad (9th generation):

Overview: The standard iPad is Apple's entry-level model, comes in classic design with a home button for navigation and thick bezels on the top and bottom. It's an excellent all-rounder and the most budget-friendly option.

Screen Size: Comes with a 10.2-inch screen, which is large enough for reading, browsing, and video calls.

Features: Supports the first gen Apple Pencil, making it great for note-taking or drawing. It has a good camera and enough power for everyday tasks.

Best For: Those who want a solid iPad experience without needing advanced features.

2. iPad (10th generation):

Overview: The 10th generation iPad is Apple's new entry-level model. It has design from more expensive models with large screen and gesture-Based Navigation.

Screen Size: Comes with a 10.9-inch screen, which is larger than 9th gen Ipad.

Features: Supports the first gen Apple Pencil, making it great for note-taking or drawing. It has a great camera and enough power for everyday tasks.

Best For: Those who want to get a modern design iPad without needing advanced features.

3. iPad Mini:

Overview: As the name suggests, the iPad Mini is the smallest in the lineup. It's compact and lightweight, perfect for those who prioritize portability.

Screen Size: Has an 8.3-inch screen. Despite its smaller size, the screen is sharp and vibrant.

Features: it supports the second-generation Apple Pencil. It's powerful for its size and can handle most tasks effortlessly.

Best For: Seniors who are always on the go or prefer a smaller device that's easy to hold for long periods.

4. iPad Air:

Overview: The iPad Air is a step up in terms of performance and features. It has a similar design to 10th gen, but more powerful internals and better screen quality.

Screen Size: Comes with a 10.9-inch Liquid Retina display, offering a more comfortable experience with apple pencil.

Features: Supports the second-generation Apple Pencil, has a better camera system, and includes advanced features like Stage Manager for multitasking.

Best For: Those who want a bit more power and sophistication from their iPad, perfect for creative hobbies or more intensive use.

5. iPad Pro:

Overview: The iPad Pro is the top-tier model, offering the most advanced features. It's aimed at professionals or those who want the best of the best.

Screen Sizes: Available in two sizes – 11-inch and 12.9-inch. The 12.9-inch model has a Liquid Retina XDR display, which is the best display available on an iPad.

Features: It's the most powerful iPad, great for demanding apps and tasks. Supports the second-generation Apple Pencil, has the best camera system, and includes features like Face ID.

Best For: Tech enthusiasts or seniors who want a device for complex tasks like video editing, professional art, or those who just want the premium iPad experience.

- Key features and specifications of each model, explained in layman's terms.

When choosing the right iPad, it's essential to consider what feels most comfortable and meets your needs. If you're fond of the traditional design with a physical Home button, the 9th generation iPad stands as your sole option, offering the familiarity and ease of a classic iPad experience.

For many, the 10th generation iPad, being the new standard model, strikes a perfect balance of features and usability, catering well to a broad range of everyday needs.

If portability is a priority, the iPad Mini is wonderfully compact, although this smaller size does mean a shorter battery life, something to keep in mind if you're away from a charger for extended periods.

For those who enjoy a finer screen quality, perhaps for drawing or viewing photos, the iPad Air presents a notable upgrade in display compared to the 10th generation, with enhanced compatibility with the Apple Pencil.

For professionals who might require more advanced capabilities, particularly for tasks like graphic design or video editing, the iPad Pro 11 inches becomes a necessity, offering top-tier performance and features.

Lastly, the iPad Pro 12.9 inches, with its expansive screen, is more suited for stationary use at home, perhaps as a replacement for a traditional desktop computer, due to its considerable size.

In summary, each iPad model has its unique strengths and considerations. Whether it's the comfort of a Home button, the ease of a standard model, the portability of a Mini, the enhanced display of an Air, or the professional-grade capabilities of a Pro, your choice should align with how you plan to use your iPad in your daily life.

- Guidance on choosing the right amount of memory for your iPad

When it comes to choosing the right amount of memory for your iPad, it's essential to consider your specific needs. Currently, Apple offers iPads mainly in two memory sizes: 64GB and 256GB. The iPad Pro, catering to more demanding users, extends its range from 128GB to a large 2TB.

For older individuals, who might use their iPad for browsing the web, reading, light gaming, and staying connected with family through photos and videos, the storage requirements are generally moderate. In most cases, 64GB should suffice for these activities. However, if you have a passion for photography or like to keep a large collection of videos and photos, opting for a 256GB model would be a prudent choice to avoid running out of space.

The average tablet user, according to general usage patterns, might find 128GB a balanced option. It offers ample space for a variety of apps, documents, and media, without the premium cost of higher-capacity models. For instance, a study or survey might indicate that users with diverse interests, from gaming to media consumption, find 128GB accommodating their needs comfortably. However, the base 64GB model can also be adequate, especially if your usage revolves around streaming content online without the need to store large files on the device itself.

Therefore, when selecting your iPad, assess how you plan to use it. If your usage is light to moderate, 64GB should be enough. For those with higher storage demands, like extensive media libraries or professional tasks, considering 256GB or more, especially in the iPad Pro range, would be a wise choice. Remember, it's about balancing your needs with the cost, ensuring that you get the most value and functionality from your iPad.

1.3 Terminology

In this section, we present a concise overview of the basic terms you'll encounter throughout this book. Don't worry about memorizing them all at once; we'll revisit and explain each term in more detail in the relevant chapters later on. Think of this as a quick introduction, a primer to the language of iPads, designed to make your journey through the rest of the book more comfortable and understandable.

- iPadOS: The special software that runs on your iPad.
- Apple ID: Your personal key to use Apple services like the App Store.
- App Store: A place on your iPad where you can download new applications.
- Apple Pay: A way to pay for things using your iPad securely.
- Bluetooth: A feature to connect your iPad wirelessly to other devices, like headphones.
- Wi-Fi: The wireless connection that gives you access to the internet.
- iCloud: Apple's online storage where you can keep your photos and documents safe.
- Siri: A voice-activated helper on your iPad for questions and commands.

- Touch ID/Face ID: Security features to unlock your iPad using your fingerprint or face.
- AirDrop: A quick way to send photos and files to other Apple devices nearby.
- Home Button: A physical button on older iPads to go back to the main screen.
- Gesture Control: Using finger movements on the screen to control your iPad.
- Lock Screen: The first screen you see when you turn on or wake up your iPad.
- Home Screen: The main screen where all your apps are displayed.
- Control Center: A menu for quick access to frequently used settings.
- Notification Center: Where all your recent alerts and messages show up.
- Dock: A row of your favorite apps at the bottom of the Home Screen.
- Spotlight Search: A tool to help you find almost anything on your iPad.
- Screenshot: Taking a picture of what's on your iPad screen.
- Sync: Making sure the same information is on your iPad and other devices.
- Force Quit: A way to close an app that isn't working correctly.

1.4 How to Use This Book

We will walk you through each of the main functions of your iPad, explaining what they are and how they can be used in your daily life. Our aim is to help you not only understand the basic features but also to utilize your tablet to its fullest potential, exploring all the wonderful things it can do.

To make this learning process smooth, we've structured the book in a way that starts with the simplest concepts and gradually moves to more complex ones. This step-by-step approach ensures that you build a solid foundation of knowledge and confidence as you progress through the book.

If you are new to using an iPad, we recommend that you go through the book chapter by chapter, following the instructions in the order they are presented. This methodical approach will help you gain a comprehensive understanding of your iPad rather than jumping straight to a specific section that might interest you. By taking it one step at a time, you'll find that the journey of learning about your iPad is both rewarding and enjoyable.

So, let's begin this adventure together, and soon you'll be using your iPad like a pro, discovering all the amazing things it has to offer!

Chapter 2: Getting Started with Your iPad

2.1 Charging/Turning on/ IO - Physical Buttons

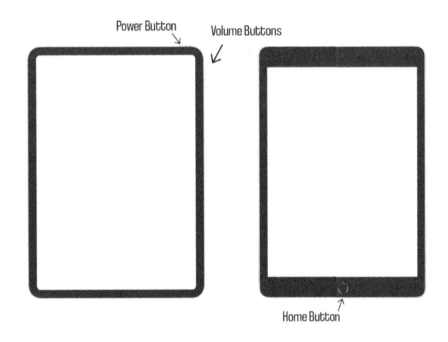

Your iPad, a sleek and elegant device, comes with a few key physical controls. These are simple buttons and ports designed to be user-friendly. You'll find a **power button**, which is used for turning your iPad on or off. This button is also useful for waking your iPad up from sleep mode or putting it back to sleep. Along the side of your iPad, there are **volume buttons** that control how loud or soft any sound from your iPad is, be it during a video call or while watching a movie.

Cameras on Your iPad

Your iPad has cameras for taking photos and video chatting. The primary camera unit is on the back. This is what you'll use for taking pictures of things around you. There's also a camera on the front, above the screen, for when you want to talk to family and friends on video calls.

Turning On Your iPad

To start your iPad, press and hold the power button for a few seconds. You'll see an apple, like the fruit, appear on the screen - that means it's turning on. When you see your home screen, it's ready to use.

Charging Your iPad

Now, let's make sure your iPad has power. Your iPad and its charger both use a Type-C cable. This means the plug looks the same on both ends. Find the charging port on your iPad - it's a small slot. Plug one end of the cable in here, and the other end into the charger, then plug the charger into a wall socket. A small battery picture on your iPad's screen will show it's charging. You can still use your iPad while it's plugged in.

2.2 New iPad User. Apple ID Creation

- Setting Up Your iPad

Setting up your new iPad is an exciting first step in your journey with this wonderful device. Let's go through this process together, step by step. Remember, take your time and don't rush - it's all about making your iPad work just right for you.

1. Power On Your iPad

Start by pressing and holding the top button until the Apple logo appears on the screen.
Wait for a few moments as your iPad starts up.

2. Welcome Screen and Language Selection

Once your iPad turns on, you'll see a "Hello" in different languages.
Swipe up from the bottom of the screen to start.
Choose your language and your country or region from the lists.

3. Connect to Wi-Fi

Your iPad will ask you to choose a Wi-Fi network.
Tap the name of your Wi-Fi network and enter the password if required.

4. Set Up Face ID or Touch ID

If your iPad supports Face ID or Touch ID, it will ask you to set this up.
Follow the on-screen instructions to scan your face or fingerprint.
This feature helps keep your iPad secure. And will make many interactions with your Apple ID easier, so please don't skip this part

5. Create or Sign In with an Apple ID

If you already have an Apple ID, enter your email and password to sign in.
If you don't have an Apple ID, the iPad will guide you through creating one.
The process of creating an Apple ID is covered in detail in the following section

6. Agree to Terms and Conditions

Read through the terms and conditions (or at least glance through them).
Tap "Agree" to proceed.

7. Set Up iCloud and Find My iPad

iCloud lets you store photos, documents, and backups online.
Find My iPad can help you locate your device if it gets lost.
You can choose to enable these features or skip them for now.

8. Enable Location Services

Location services allow apps like Maps to know where you are.
You can turn this on or choose to keep it off for privacy reasons.

9. Finalize Settings

You might be asked to set up Siri, Apple's voice assistant, and other services.
Go through each step, choosing your preferences.

10. Welcome to the Home Screen

Once everything is set up, you'll be taken to your Home Screen.
This is where all your apps will be.

- A walkthrough for new users on setting up an Apple ID.

An Apple ID is your personal account used for everything you do with Apple, like downloading apps from the App Store, backing up your iPad data to iCloud, and making purchases.

Before we start creating your Apple ID, it's a good idea to first read and understand each step in the guide. Don't hurry to make your Apple ID right away. Take a look at the next section about security first. Once you know all this, you'll be ready to set up your Apple ID.

- Start from the Welcome Screen

  - During your iPad setup, you'll reach a screen asking for an Apple ID. Here, you can either log in with an existing Apple ID or create a new one.

- Creating a New Apple ID

  - Tap 'Forgot password or don't have an Apple ID?'
  - Select 'Create a Free Apple ID.'

- Enter Your Details

  - Fill in your name and birthday.
  - Next, you'll be asked to enter your email address. This will be your new Apple ID. Make sure to use an email address that you regularly check.

- Choose a Strong Password

  - Create a password for your Apple ID. It should be strong and unique, with a mix of letters, numbers, and symbols.
  - You'll need to enter this password twice to confirm it.

- Security Questions

  - Choose and answer a few security questions. These questions are important as they help to keep your account secure and assist you in recovering your account if you forget your password.

- Phone Number and Communication Preferences

  - Enter a phone number for additional account security.
  - Decide if you want to receive email updates from Apple.

- Agree to the Terms and Conditions

  - Read the terms and conditions and tap 'Agree.' You might need to tap 'Agree' again in a pop-up window.

- Verification and Completion

    - Apple will send a verification code to the email address you provided. Check your email, find the code, and enter it on your iPad.
    - Once verified, your Apple ID is set up and ready to use!

Security

As you set up your new iPad and Apple ID, it's crucial to ensure that all your personal information is entered safely and kept secure. Here are some guidelines to help you protect your information during and after the setup process.

1. Create a Strong and Unique Password

Your Apple ID password is the key to your account. Make sure it's strong – use a combination of letters (both upper and lower case), numbers, and symbols.
Avoid using easily guessable information like birthdays, anniversaries, or common words.

2. Be Mindful of Security Questions

Choose security questions that are memorable to you but not easily guessable by others.
The answers to your security questions add an extra layer of security to your account.

3. Use a Reliable Email Address

Your Apple ID is linked to your email address. Use an email account that you regularly access and is secured with a strong password.

4. Verify Your Contact Information

Make sure the phone number and email address you provide are accurate. Thes are essential for recovering your account if you ever forget your password.

5. Keep Your Software Updated

After setting up your iPad, regularly check for and install software updates. Thes updates often include important security improvements.

6. Beware of Phishing Attempts

Be cautious of unsolicited emails or messages asking for your Apple ID or othe personal information. Apple will never ask for this information in an email.

7. Two-Factor Authentication

Consider enabling two-factor authentication for your Apple ID for added securit This requires both your password and an additional piece of information to log in t your account.

8. Logging Out on Shared Devices

If you ever need to log in to your Apple ID on a device that isn't yours, alway remember to log out when you're done.

2.3 Previous iPad Owner

- Instructions on transferring information from an old iPad to a new one.

If you're upgrading from an older iPad to a new one, transferring your information is a key step. This process ensures that all your apps, settings, and personal conten are moved over to your new device seamlessly. Let's walk through how to do thi effectively.

Transferring Information from an Old iPad to a New One

1. Backup Your Old iPad

Before starting, make sure your old iPad is backed up. You can do this using iCloud or your computer. To backup with iCloud, go to Settings, tap your name, then iCloud, and finally select 'iCloud Backup' to make sure it's turned on and tap 'Back Up Now.'

2. Start Your New iPad

Turn on your new iPad and place it near your old one. You should see a prompt on the old iPad asking if you want to set up a new device. Tap 'Continue.'

3. Use Quick Start

A camera view will open on your old iPad. Hold it over your new iPad to scan the animation that appears on the new iPad's screen. This will pair your devices.

4. Enter Your Passcode

You'll be asked to enter your old iPad's passcode on your new one. This step is part of Apple's security measures.

5. Set Up Face ID or Touch ID

Follow the instructions to set up Face ID or Touch ID on your new iPad.

6. Transfer Your Data

You'll be given the option to transfer your data. You can choose to transfer from the iCloud backup or directly from your old iPad.

7. Wait for the Transfer to Complete

Keep the two devices near each other and connected to Wi-Fi. The transfer time will depend on how much data you have.

8. Finish the Setup

Once the transfer is complete, you can finish setting up your new iPad by following the remaining on-screen instructions.

By following these steps, you can smoothly transition to your new iPad without losing your important data and settings. It's a simple process that ensures your new iPad feels familiar right from the start, with all your apps, photos, and personal settings in place.

2.4 Sync with iPhone

Having your iPad and iPhone in sync can make your life much easier. It ensures that your important information, like contacts, photos, and documents, are the same on both devices. Let's go through a step-by-step guide to help you sync your iPad with your iPhone.

Step-by-step guide on how to sync your iPad with your iPhone.

- Ensure Both Devices are Using the Same Apple ID

  - To sync your iPad and iPhone, they both need to be signed in to the same Apple ID. Check this in the Settings app under your name at the top.

- Connect to Wi-Fi and Enable Bluetooth

  - Ensure your iPad and iPhone are connected to Wi-Fi and have Bluetooth turned on. This helps in the syncing process.

- Turn On iCloud Sync for Various Services

    - Go to Settings, tap your name, and then tap 'iCloud.' Here, you'll see a list of services like Photos, Contacts, and Calendars.

- Ensure the switches next to these services are turned on. This will sync this data between your iPad and iPhone.

- Sync Your Photos

    - To sync your photos, select 'Photos' in the iCloud settings and turn on 'iCloud Photos.' This keeps your photos and videos updated across both devices.

- Use Handoff to Continue Tasks Across Devices

    - Handoff allows you to start a task on one device and continue it on another. To use Handoff, go to Settings > General > Handoff and make sure it's turned on for both devices.

- Set Up iCloud Keychain for Password Sync

    - If you want to sync your passwords, turn on the iCloud Keychain by going to Settings > [your name] > iCloud > Keychain and toggle it on.

- Syncing Messages and Calls

    - To sync your messages, go to Settings > Messages and tap on 'Text Message Forwarding.' Here, enable your iPad.
    - For calls, go to Settings > Phone > Calls on Other Devices and enable your iPad.

- Check for Consistency

  - After setting everything up, check a few items like contacts or notes to ensur they synced properly between your iPad and iPhone.

In upcoming chapters we'll explore how to use iCloud beyond just syncing covering its various features, how to manage your storage, and tips for keeping you data secure in the cloud.

2.5 Security and Privacy

- Overview of the security features available on the iPad (Touch ID, Face ID).

As you enjoy your iPad, you'll appreciate how Touch ID and Face ID make using not only more secure but also much easier, especially when it comes to everyda tasks.

Touch ID is a feature found on most iPads, including the 9th generation iPad wit the Home button and other models with it on the power button. It uses you fingerprint to unlock your iPad. This means you don't have to type in your passwor every time you want to use it – just place your finger on the button, and you're in. It' that simple. Plus, when downloading apps or making purchases, Touch ID means yo can just use your fingerprint instead of typing in your Apple ID password each time

For those with an iPad Pro, there's Face ID. It uses your face as the key to unloc your iPad. Just look at your iPad, and it unlocks automatically. It's really convenient i you find remembering passwords a bit of a hassle or if typing them in is becomin difficult. Face ID can also be used for quick access to banking apps and other secur applications, making it not only a safe option but a very handy one.

Both these features are about making your iPad as easy to use as possible.

- How to set up and use these features.

If you didn't set up Touch ID or Face ID when you first started using your iPad, don't worry. You can easily set them up anytime. Here's how to do it in a few simple steps:

Setting Up Touch ID:

- Find Settings: Tap on the 'Settings' app on your iPad.
- Go to Touch ID & Passcode: In the Settings menu, find and tap on 'Touch ID & Passcode.' You might need to enter your passcode if you have one.
- Add a Fingerprint: Tap on 'Add a Fingerprint.' Follow the instructions, which will ask you to place and lift your finger on the Home button or power button several times.
- Complete the Process: Follow the on-screen instructions until your fingerprint is fully captured. You can add more than one fingerprint if you like.

Setting Up Face ID:

- Open Settings: On your iPad Pro, open the 'Settings' app.
- Select Face ID & Passcode: Look for 'Face ID & Passcode' in the settings list and tap on it. Enter your passcode if prompted.
- Set Up Face ID: Tap 'Set Up Face ID.' Hold your iPad in portrait mode and position your face in front of your device. Follow the on-screen instructions, which will guide you to move your head in a circle so the camera can recognize your face.
- Finish the Setup: Once your face is scanned, Face ID is set up and ready to use.

Chapter 3: Basics

3.1 Lockscreen Customization

- How to change the wallpaper on your lock screen for personalization.

The lock screen on your iPad is simple but useful. It shows you the time and date right away. You can also add small tools, called widgets, to get quick updates. You can change the background picture to something you like. When you get messages or alerts, they show up here too. This chapter will help you understand and set up your lock screen..

- Starting the Customization Process:

- To begin, touch and hold the lock screen of your iPad. A 'Customize' option and an 'Add New' button should appear at the bottom of the screen. If they don't, try holding the lock screen again and then enter your passcode.

- Selecting a New Lock Screen:

- Tap on the 'Add New' button to create a new lock screen. You can choose from various wallpaper options displayed, including photos and suggested images by Apple.

- Customizing the Time Display:

  - You can tap on the time displayed on the lock screen to change its font, color, and style. A slider may be available to adjust the font weight, depending on your font choice.

- Adding Widgets:

  - Widgets are small information blocks that can display data like the weather, calendar events, or news headlines. To add widgets, tap 'Add Widgets' or the date. In landscape orientation, you can add widgets on the left side of the screen, while in portrait orientation, you can add them below or above the time.

- Finalizing Your Customization:

  - After you have made your choices, tap 'Add' or 'Done'. You can then set your creation as the wallpaper for both the lock screen and home screen, or further customize the home screen if desired.

3.2 Homescreen Customization

- Steps to rearrange, add, and delete app icons on the home screen.

The home screen of your iPad is like your personal command center. It ha everything you need at your fingertips: apps, widgets for quick information, th current time, a dock at the bottom for your favorite apps, and multiple pages you ca swipe through. This is where you launch apps and see important info at a glance Let's explore how you can rearrange apps, add widgets, and personalize your hom screen to suit your style and needs.

To move an app, just touch and hold its icon until it wiggles, then drag it to wher you want it. If you want to add more apps, you can download them from the Ap Store. To remove an app you no longer need, touch and hold the app and ta 'Delete.'

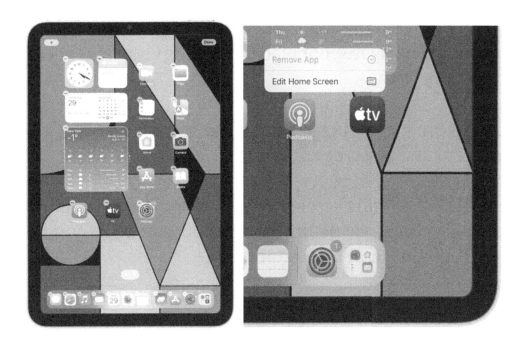

You can also change the background of your home screen to make it more personal. Go to your Settings, tap 'Wallpaper,' and then choose a new wallpaper. You can select one of the many options Apple provides or use a photo from your own collection. Just tap 'Set' after choosing, and your wallpaper will change.

3.3 Understanding App Icons

App icons on your iPad are like little doors that open up into different tools and games. Each icon represents a different app, and the picture on the icon usually gives you a hint about what the app does. For example, the icon with a camera takes you to the app where you can take photos. The envelope icon opens your email, and the blue compass icon is where you can browse the internet. Recognizing these common icons helps you navigate your iPad more easily, as you learn which apps do what just by looking at their pictures.

3.4 Gestures

- Introduction to basic iPad gestures for navigation, like swiping and pinching.

Using your iPad involves learning a few simple finger movements called gestures. These gestures let you navigate your iPad by swiping your finger across the screen or pinching with two fingers.

- Swipe: Gently drag your finger across the screen. Use this to scroll through a webpage or move between screens.

  - To go back to the home screen, swipe up from the bottom edge of the screen.
  - To see recent apps, swipe up from the bottom edge and hold your finger in the middle of the screen for a moment.

- Pinch: Place two fingers on the screen and move them together or apart. This gesture is used to zoom in or out on photos, maps, or web pages.

- Tap: Lightly touch the screen with your finger to open apps, select items, or enter text. It's like pointing and clicking with a mouse.

- Double Tap: Quickly tap twice on the screen. In some apps, like the Photos app, this will zoom in and then zoom out again.

- Rotate: Place two fingers on an item, such as a photo, and twist them. This rotates the item.

Remember, these gestures are designed to be intuitive. With some practice, you'll find they become second nature, making navigating your iPad a breeze.

There are a lot more features available with gestures on the tablet:

Quick App Switching: For a swift switch between open apps, swipe left or right along the bottom edge of the screen. It's as easy as flipping through pages in a magazine to find your place.

Showing the Dock in an App: When in an app, swipe up slightly from the bottom edge of the screen to reveal the Dock. This allows you to open another app without returning to the home screen.

Opening Siri: Activate Siri by holding down the Top (or Side) button until Siri shows up

Taking a Screenshot: Simultaneously press and then quickly release the Top (or Side) button and the Volume Up button

Turning Off the iPad: Press and hold the Volume button and the Top (or Side) button until you see the power off slider. Slide to power off, similar to turning off a television with a remote.

Force Restart of iPad: quickly press and release the Volume Up button, then the Volume Down button. Next, press and hold the Top button until the device restarts.

Accessing the Control Center: Swipe down from the top-right corner of your screen to open the Control Center, providing quick access to settings like brightness and volume

Quick Notes: swipe up from the bottom-right corner of the screen. This action will open a new Quick Note

3.5 Control Center

- How to access and use the Control Center for quick settings adjustments.

The Control Center is a handy feature on your iPad that gives you quick access to various settings and functions, making it easier to use your device.

To open the Control Center, simply swipe down from the upper-right corner of the screen. Once opened, you can tap on the different icons to toggle functions like Wi-Fi, Bluetooth, and brightness. The standard functions also include music controls, screen orientation lock, and volume control.

To add new functions or organize the Control Center, go to 'Settings' and then 'Control Center.' Here, you can customize it by adding additional controls like Flashlight or Camera and arranging them to suit your preferences.

- Customizing the Control Center to include the tools you use most often.

Control Center also has hidden functions that are revealed when you long press o specific icons:

- Display Settings: Pressing and holding the brightness slider lets you access True Tone, Dark Mode, and Night Shift. True Tone adjusts your display to your environment's lighting, Dark Mode is easier on the eyes in low light, and Night Shift reduces blue light at night.
- Wi-Fi Networks: Long-pressing the Wi-Fi icon lets you quickly switch between networks.
- Flashlight Brightness: Adjust the intensity of the flashlight by long-pressing its icon.
- Music Controls: A long press on the music icon expands the control for more detailed music playback options, including volume adjustments and track changes.

3.6 Wi-Fi Connection

- Connecting to a Wi-Fi Network

  - To connect your iPad to Wi-Fi, first, tap the 'Settings' icon on your hom screen.
  - In Settings, tap 'Wi-Fi.'
  - Make sure Wi-Fi is turned on, then a list of available networks will appear.
  - Select your network. If it's secured, you'll need to enter the password.
  - Once entered, your iPad will connect, and a checkmark will appear next to th network name.

- Troubleshooting Common Issues

  - If you can't see your network, make sure your router is on and working.
  - If you can't connect, check to make sure you entered the correct password.
  - If you're still having trouble, try turning Wi-Fi off and on again in the Settings.
  - Restarting your iPad can also help resolve connection issues.

3.7 Cellular Connection

If your iPad has cellular capabilities, you can connect to the internet even when you're not near Wi-Fi.

- Setting Up Cellular Data

  - Go to 'Settings' and tap 'Cellular Data' or 'Mobile Data.'
  - Turn on 'Cellular Data' to activate your connection.
  - If you need to add a cellular plan, follow the on-screen instructions or contact your carrier.

- Managing Your Connection

  - You can turn cellular data on or off for specific apps under 'Settings' > 'Cellular Data.'
  - Keep an eye on your data usage in the same menu to avoid overcharges.

3.8 Bluetooth

Bluetooth lets you wirelessly connect your iPad to devices like headphones, speakers, or keyboards.

- Turning on Bluetooth

  - Open 'Settings' and tap 'Bluetooth.'
  - Switch 'Bluetooth' on. Your iPad will start searching for nearby devices.

- Pairing a Device

  - Ensure the device you want to connect with is in pairing mode.
  - It should appear under 'Other Devices' on your iPad. Tap its name to pair.
  - If asked for a code, enter the one provided with your device.

- Managing Bluetooth Devices

  - Once paired, devices will be listed under 'My Devices.'
  - Tap a device name for options like disconnecting or forgetting the device.

Chapter 4: How to Simplify the Use of the iPad

In this chapter, we'll embark on a journey to make your iPad more personal and convenient for you. Just like adding a personal touch to your living room or customizing your morning routine, we'll tailor your iPad to fit your lifestyle perfectly. From adjusting text sizes to suit your vision to organizing your apps and widgets for easy access, each step is designed to enhance your iPad experience. We'll also introduce you to Siri, your digital assistant, and explore the wonders of AirDrop. Let's dive in and transform your iPad into your most helpful and enjoyable companion!

4.1 Change Font Size

If reading text on your iPad feels like reading a distant street sign without your glasses, here's a quick fix. Go to 'Settings,' tap 'Display & Brightness,' and then 'Text Size.' Here, you can slide to increase or decrease the text size. The bigger text means no more squinting!

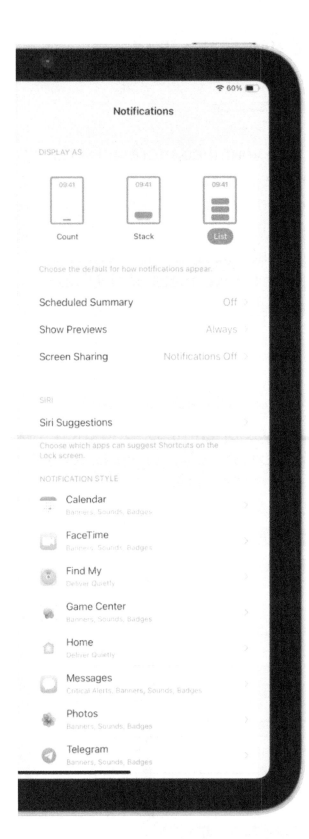

4.2 Notifications

Notifications are like little digital nudges. T[o] manage these, head to 'Settings' and ta[p] 'Notifications.' Here, you can choose whic[h] apps can send you notifications and how the[y] appear, so you only get the nudges you real[ly] want.

When customizing notifications on your iPa[d] consider your daily activities and preference[s] to decide which notifications to enable [or] disable:

• Enable Notifications for Importar[t] Apps: Keep notifications turned on f[or] messaging apps, email, and social network[s] if staying connected with family and friends [is] important to you. These notifications ensur[e] you don't miss important messages [or] updates.

• Disable Game Notifications: If yo[u] have games on your iPad, you might want t[o] turn off their notifications. They can b[e] frequent and distracting, especially if you on[ly] play games occasionally.

Remember, the goal is to make your iPa[d] experience more pleasant and les[s] overwhelming. By carefully selecting whic[h] notifications to receive, you can keep you[r] focus on what matters most to you.

4.3 Keyboard Settings

• Adding Keyboards:

  • Go to 'Settings,' tap 'General,' then 'Keyboard,' and select 'Keyboards.'
Tap 'Add New Keyboard' to include different language keyboards, the emoji keyboard, or even third-party keyboards.

• Shortcut Dictionary:

In the 'Keyboard' settings, you can also add shortcuts for phrases you use frequently on 'Text Replacement' menu.

• Changing Languages:

  • While typing, tap the globe icon to switch languages. Holding it down brings up your list of keyboards.

• Hidden Keyboard Functions:

  • Move the cursor by pressing and holding the spacebar, then sliding your finger.

- Type by sliding from one letter to another on the keyboard, a feature called 'Slide to Type.'

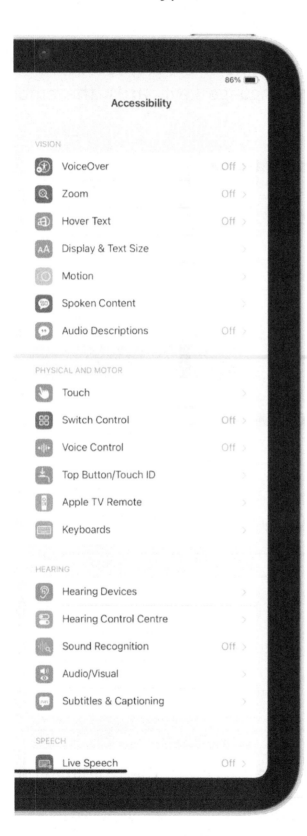

4.4 Accessibility Features for Seniors

The iPad offers a range of accessibility features designed to make it easier and more enjoyable for seniors.

- VoiceOver: Ideal for those with visual impairments. Activate it in 'Settings' under 'Accessibility.' VoiceOver reads aloud what's on your screen. Control it by gestures and use Siri to enable it by saying, "Turn on VoiceOver."

- Zoom Feature: It is a useful tool for enlarging what's on your screen. To activate Zoom, head to 'Settings,' select 'Accessibility,' and then tap 'Zoom.' Once enabled, you can double-tap with three fingers to zoom in or out.

You can personalize your Zoom experience with several options:

- Follow Focus: Adjust the zoom to follow your selections.
- Smart Typing: Zooms in when typing and out when finished.
- Zoom Filter: Apply different color filters for easier viewing.

- Keyboard Shortcuts: Handy shortcuts for quick zoom adjustments.
- Zoom Controller: An on-screen controller for easy zoom manipulation.
- Zoom Region: Choose between full screen or window zoom.
- Show While Mirroring: Decide if zoom should be active during screen sharing.

At the bottom of the Zoom settings, you'll find a slider to adjust the maximum zoom level. This feature makes your iPad more accessible, especially when reading or viewing detailed content.

- Hover Text: Great for reading small text. Enable it in 'Accessibility.' It displays a high-resolution zoom of text, fields, menu items, buttons, and more.

- Reducing Motion Effects: Beneficial for those who are sensitive to motion and screen movement. Turn it off in 'Accessibility' to reduce the motion of the user interface, including the parallax effect of icons.

- Spoken Content: Useful for those who benefit from auditory reading. Activate it in 'Accessibility.' It reads aloud text on the screen.

- Hearing Accessibility Options:
    - Sound Recognition: Notifies you of certain sounds like doorbells or alarms.
    - Audio and Visual: Offers visual alerts and balance controls.
    - Live Captions: For real-time captioning of conversations.

- Live Speech: allows you to type words and have them spoken aloud, which is especially useful in FaceTime calls or communication apps. Activate it by turning on Live Speech in 'Settings' and then triple-tapping the power button. You can even personalize it with your favorite phrases and choose from a variety of voices.

    - Personal Voice, a new feature found under 'Settings' > 'Accessibility,' lets you record up to 150 phrases for different situations. This is particularly helpful if you have difficulty speaking. Your Personal Voice can be managed with options like continuing recording, exporting, and deleting voice recordings.

Together, Live Speech and Personal Voice provide a unique way to communicate allowing you to speak through typed text and pre-recorded phrases.

● Assistive Access: For those with limited physical mobility. Activate in 'Accessibility to customize touch settings, create shortcuts, and control your iPad with minima physical interaction.

4.5 Homescreen Customization, Folders

Think of your home screen as a digital garden. You can organize your apps int folders by dragging them together. Widgets, like little info panels, can be added fc weather updates or news.

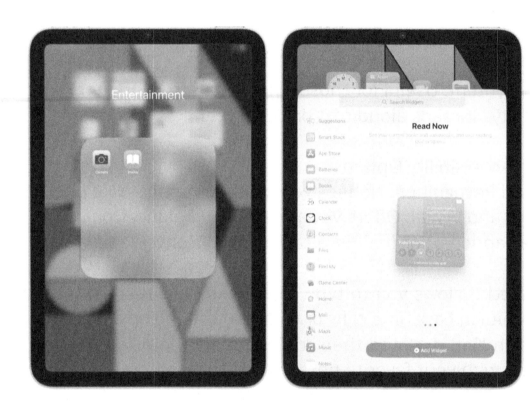

Widgets offer several advantages over regular app icons, particularly in term of functionality and convenience:

- Live Updates: Widgets provide real-time information or updates. For example, a weather widget can show the current temperature and forecast without needing to open the app.
- Quick Access: Widgets often allow for quicker interactions with apps. You can, for instance, play music, check your calendar, or see to-do lists directly from the home screen.
- Larger Display: Widgets are larger than icons, making them easier to read and interact with, especially for those who might find small text challenging.

Consider adding large weather widgets to the top of your home screen for easy visibility of daily forecasts

Creating folders for your apps is simple: just drag similar apps together. This organization reduces clutter and makes finding apps easier.

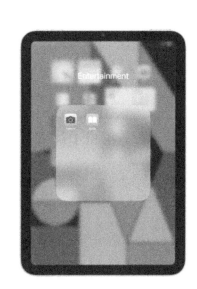

The dock at the bottom of your screen is perfect for your most-used apps. Try to limit the number of apps in the dock to around four or five. This prevents icons from becoming too small and ensures easy access. This setup transforms your home screen into an organized, senior-friendly interface, tailored to your needs and interests.

Customizing the Dock:

- To add an app to the Dock, touch and hold an app icon until it wiggles, then drag it down to the Dock.
- To remove an app from the Dock, drag it out of the Dock and onto the home screen.
- Remember, there's limited space, so choose the apps you use the most, like your email, calendar, or favorite game.

Siri Recommendations in the Dock show apps that Siri suggests based on you usage patterns. It's like having a personal assistant who hands you the right tool jus as you need it. These recommendations change throughout the day based on you habits. For example, if you check the news every morning, the News app migh appear in your Dock in the morning hours.

App Library Introduced in recent iPadOS updates, it automatically organizes al your apps into categories. It's like having a bookshelf where all your books (apps) are neatly sorted into genres.

4.6 Talk to Siri

Siri is your digital assistant, always ready to help.

- Activating Siri: Press and hold the Home button (or the top button on newer models) until Siri appears. You may need to activate it before the first run Just press "Turn on Siri"

-

- Speaking to Siri: Just talk as you would to a person. Say things like "What's the weather today?" or "Remind me to call John at 3 PM."

- Asking Questions: You can ask Siri for directions, set alarms, open apps, or even get answers to general questions.

- Dictation: Besides asking questions, you can use Siri to dictate messages or notes. Just tap the microphone icon on the keyboard and start speaking.

- Accessibility: Siri can read emails, send messages, and more, which is particularly helpful for those with vision or mobility challenges.

Remember, Siri is designed to be user-friendly, so don't hesitate to experiment and ask different questions to get the most out of this feature.

4.7 AirDrop

AirDrop is like a magic trick for sharing photos or documents. Swipe down from the top-right to open the Control Center, tap on 'AirDrop,' and choose who can send you items. To share something, tap the 'Share' icon, then choose AirDrop and the recipient.

Chapter 5: Discovering Apps Included with Your iPad

5.1 Key Takeaway

Welcome to the magical world of your new iPad, much like opening a treasur chest full of gems – in this case, apps. Yes, your iPad comes pre-installed with variety of applications, each ready to add convenience and fun to your day.

Each app is designed to enrich your daily life, turning your iPad into not just device, but a versatile companion in your digital adventures.

5.2 Common Apps

Your 'Photos' app is a digital photo album, holding cherished memories. Wit 'Maps,' navigate new routes like a seasoned explorer. 'Books' is your personal library offering stories and knowledge. Enjoy melodies and podcasts in 'Music,' which is lik having a concert in your hands

5.3 Navigation

Navigating apps on your iPad is quite straightforward. To open an app, just tap it icon on the Home screen. Inside, you'll usually find a navigation menu at the bottom To return to a previous page within the app, look for a 'back' button at the top le corner or simply swipe your finger from left to right across the screen. To close a app, press the Home button or, on newer iPads without a Home button, swipe u from the bottom edge of the screen. This intuitive design makes using apps on you iPad a breeze.

5.4 Pre-installed apps

• Photos: Stores and organizes your pictures and videos. You can edit them, create albums, and share with others.

• Viewing Photos: Your photos and videos are automatically organized. You can browse them by different categories like 'Years,' 'Months,' 'Days,' and 'All Photos.'

• Creating Albums: Group your photos into albums for better organization. Tap 'Albums,' then '+' to create a new album.

• Editing Photos: Select a photo and tap 'Edit' to adjust its look. You can crop, apply filters, and adjust lighting and color.

• Sharing Photos: Share photos via email, message, or social media by selecting a photo and tapping the 'Share' button.

• Deleting Photos: To delete, select a photo and tap the trash can icon.

The Photos app is a powerful tool for keeping your memories organized and looking their best.

• Clock: Shows the current time, and includes features like setting alarms, a stopwatch, a timer, and world clock.

• Notes: A digital notepad for writing down thoughts, creating lists, and even adding photos or sketches.

• Files: Manages your documents and files. You can browse, search, and organize all your documents.

• Home: Controls smart home devices that are compatible with Apple's HomeKit.

• FaceTime: Video and audio calling app to connect with friends and family.

• Making a Call: Tap the plus sign (+) in the upper-right corner Enter the person's phone number, email address, or name (if they're in your contacts). Then, tap 'Video' or 'Audio' to start the call

• Receiving Calls: When someone calls you on FaceTime, a notification appears. You can tap 'Accept' to start the conversation or 'Decline' if you're unavailable.

• During the Call: While on the call, you can switch to the rea camera, mute your microphone, or adjust the volume. There's also an option to pause the video.

• Ending the Call: To end the call, simply tap the red 'End button.

• Group FaceTime: You can also do group calls by adding multiple contacts when starting a call.

• Camera: Takes photos and videos. Includes features like portrait mode, panoramic shots, and various filters.

• Maps: Provides GPS navigation, traffic information, and location search.

• Reminders: Helps you create to-do lists and set reminders for tasks

• App Store: Where you download new apps and update existing ones.

 • iTunes Store: Purchase and download music, movies, and TV shows.

 • Find My: Helps locate your iPad or other Apple devices if lost or stolen.

• Locating Your Devices: The app displays the location of your Apple devices on a map. If your iPad is lost, you can play a sound, mark it as lost, or remotely erase its data.

• Finding Friends and Family: If shared, you can see the location of friends or family members.

• Sharing Your Location: You can also share your location with others for a specified time.

• Calendar: Manage your schedule with event creation, invitations, and day/week/month views.

• Viewing Your Schedule: The app shows your schedule in different views: daily, weekly, monthly, or yearly.

• Creating Events: To add an event, tap the '+' icon. Fill in details like date, time, and location. You can also set reminders.

• Adding Birthdays: Store birthdays by creating an event on the person's birth date and select 'Birthday' as the event type.

• Editing or Deleting Events: Tap an event to edit or delete it.

- iWork: Apple's suite of productivity apps, including Pages (word processing), Numbers (spreadsheets), and Keynote (presentations).

- iMovie: A video editing app to create and edit movies.

- Safari: Safari is your gateway to the internet. It's a web browse where you can search for information, visit websites, and bookma your favorite sites. It also has a private browsing mode for more secur private searches.

- Music: This app lets you listen to your music library. You can strear songs, download music for offline listening, and explore new artists ar playlists.

- Messages: Use this app for texting with friends and family. You ca send text messages, photos, videos, and even voice messages. It als supports group chats.

- Mail: Your email hub where you can send, receive, organize, an search through your emails. You can add multiple email accounts fror different providers.

- Books: A digital bookstore and e-reader. You can purchase new books, download and read free titles, or listen to audiobooks. It als allows you to highlight text and take notes as you read.

5.5 Conclusion

Apple has carefully crafted a comprehensive suite of apps to enhance your iPa experience. Each app is designed with intuition in mind, making them user-friendl and easy to navigate. As you become more familiar with these apps, you'll find the similar style and logic of use in many other apps. This consistent design across a apps simplifies your interaction with the iPad.

Chapter 6: Browsing with Safari

Welcome to the world of Safari on your iPad, where exploring the internet is like embarking on a grand adventure from the comfort of your armchair. Safari is your digital compass, guiding you to various destinations on the web.

Imagine Safari as your friendly neighborhood store, where everything you need is within reach. When you tap the Safari icon (it looks like a compass), you enter this store. Here's what you'll find:

- Address Bar: At the top, where you type in a website address like "www.example.com".
- Back and Forward buttons: To retrace your steps or move forward.
- Tabs: Think of these like pages in a book. You can have many open at once.

- Bookmarks Button: Where you keep your favorite pages.

6.1 How to Browse the Web

Browsing the web is like leafing through a magazine. You just:

- Tap Safari to open it.
- Tap the address bar at the top.
- Type what you're looking for, like "best apple pie recipe", and press 'Go'.

It's that easy! You'll be presented with pages of information, just like flipping through different magazines.

6.2 Search

To search for something, tap the address bar and type in your query, like "What's the weather today?" Think of this as asking a librarian for a specific book.

But what if you prefer asking a different librarian? That's where changing your search engine comes in. Your iPad comes with a few different 'librarians' to choose from: Google, Bing, Yahoo, DuckDuckGo, and Ecosia. Each has its unique way of finding information for you.

To change your search engine in Safari:

- Tap the 'Settings' app.

- Scroll down and tap 'Safari'.

- Tap 'Search Engine'.

- Choose your preferred search engine from the list.

Each search engine has its flavor:

- Google: The most popular one, it's like your all-knowing friend.
- Bing: Good for visual searches and rewards.
- Yahoo: Offers a comfortable and familiar format.
- DuckDuckGo: For those who prefer more privacy.
- Ecosia: Plant trees while you search – it uses its profits for reforestation!

Remember, there's no right or wrong choice here. It's all about what suits your aste. Like choosing between tea and coffee, each has its own charm!

6.3 Browsing History

Your iPad remembers where you've been, just like a diary. To see your history:

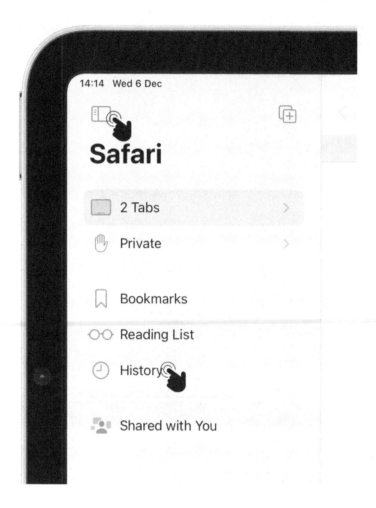

- Tap the book icon in Safari.
- Select the clock tab. Here's your browsing history!

6.4 Managing Bookmarks

Bookmarks are akin to marking your favorite pages in a book with a fold at th corner. To create a bookmark:

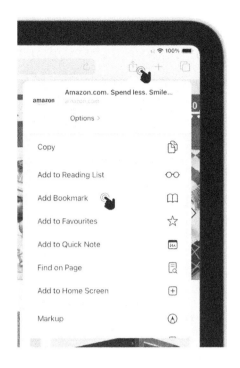

- Visit a site you like.
- Tap the share button (a square with an arrow pointing up).
- Select 'Add Bookmark'. To find it later, just tap the book icon.

6.5 Download Files

Downloading files is like picking souvenirs on a trip. To download:

- Tap a download link on a webpage.
- A message might pop up, asking if you want to download it. Tap 'Download'
- To see your downloads, tap the downloads icon (a downward arrow on a circle).

6.6 Live Text in Safari

Live Text lets you interact with text in images – like pulling a quote out of a photo. To use Live Text:

- Find an image with text in Safari.

- Press and hold the text in the image.

- Now you can copy, look up, or translate it!

6.7 Tips and Tricks to Make Browsing Easierr

- Zoom In and Out: If text is too small, pinch two fingers together on the screen and spread them apart to zoom in. Do the opposite to zoom out.

- Reader View: This removes clutter from web pages. Tap the 'AA' icon on the address bar and select 'Reader View'.

- Voice Search: Tap the microphone on the keyboard and just speak your search query.

- Split View: Want to see two things at once? Drag a tab to the side of the screen to enter Split View.

Chapter 7: App Store

Welcome to the App Store! It's like a vast library where instead of books, you find apps - those little magical tools that make your iPad even more useful. Let's walk through this digital wonderland together, step by step.

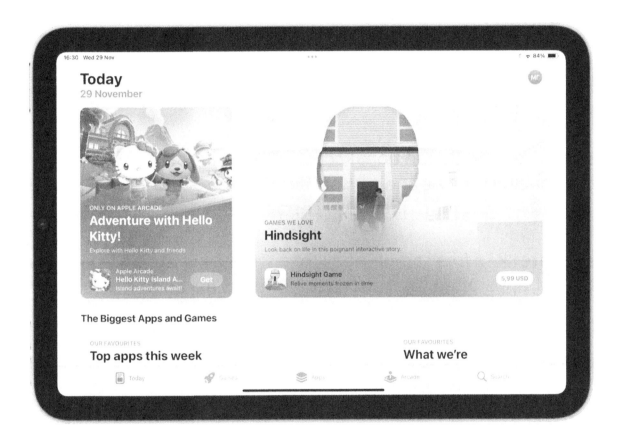

7.1 How to Download New Apps

Imagine you're in a store, picking out tools for a hobby. Here's how you do it in the App Store:

- Tap the blue 'App Store' icon on your iPad.
- At the bottom, tap 'Search' and type what you're looking for (like 'gardening').

- Browse through the options. When you find one you like, tap 'Get' (for free apps) or the price (for paid apps).
- You might need to enter your Apple ID password or use Touch ID if you've set it up.
-

SmartGym: Gym &
Home Workouts

HIIT, Home, Gym Weight L...   In-App Purchases

Get

7.2 Supporting Content

Some apps come with additional content like tutorials or extra features you can buy. It's like buying a puzzle and getting the option to buy additional pieces for a new challenge.

Free apps are like a free sample at a store, while paid apps are like buying the full product. Paid apps often offer more features or an ad-free experience, just like paying for a premium experience.

In the world of apps, you'll often come across the term '**subscription programs**' Think of these like a magazine subscription, but instead of monthly issues, you get ongoing access to an app's features or content. A subscription program in an app means paying a regular fee (monthly or yearly) to access its features, services, or content. It's becoming increasingly popular because it allows users continuous access to the latest updates, features, and support.

Apple itself offers various subscription services, enhancing your iPad experience

- Apple Music: A music streaming service with millions of songs.
- Apple TV+: A platform for movies and TV shows, including exclusive Apple content.

- Apple News+: Offers access to hundreds of magazines and leading newspapers.
- iCloud Storage Plans: To expand your storage capacity on iCloud beyond the free limit.

you'll often encounter something called **in-app purchases**. These are additional features or content you can buy within an app. It's like having the option to buy extra toppings for your ice cream after you've already bought the cone. Let's explore how you can identify and understand in-app purchases on the App Store. Look for the phrase "In-App Purchases" near the app's price or 'Get' button. This is a clear indicator that the app offers additional paid features. On the app's page in the App Store, you can usually find a section titled "In-App Purchases." This section lists the types of purchases available, such as unlocking full game levels, buying virtual currency, or subscribing to premium content.

7.3 How to Use the App Store

Navigating the App Store is like browsing a catalog:

- Today Tab: Discover new apps and read interesting stories about apps developers.
- Games and Apps Tabs: These are like different sections in a bookstore, one for games and one for other apps.
- Search Tab: Use this to find specific apps.

Apps Tab – Your Personalized Shopping Aisle

When you tap on the 'Apps' tab, you're entering a world full of various applications each designed to make life a bit easier or more enjoyable. Here's how it's organized

- Today's Picks: At the top, you'll find a selection of apps recommended by the App Store team. It's like the staff picks in a bookstore.
- New Apps We Love: Discover new and exciting apps that have just hit the shelves.
- Top Categories: This section divides apps into categories like 'Education' 'Entertainment', 'Finance', and more. It's like different genres in a bookstore
- Essentials List – The Must-Haves

I highly recommend checking out the 'Essentials' list. These apps are like the classi books everyone should have in their library. They're tried and true apps that many people find useful.

Viewing Apps by Category – Your Guided Tour

If you're looking for something specific, viewing apps by category is the way to go It's like going to a specific section in a bookstore. Here's how you do it:

- Tap the 'Apps' tab in the App Store.
- Scroll down until you see 'Top Categories'.

- Choose a category that interests you, like 'Health & Fitness' or 'Travel'.
- You'll then see a curated list of apps in that category.

This method helps you find what you're looking for much faster. Think of it as asking a librarian to guide you to a particular section rather than wandering through the whole library.

7.4 Top Social Media Apps

Stay connected with friends and family:

- Facebook: Like a town square where everyone meets.
- Instagram: A photo album where people share their life in pictures.
- Twitter: Like reading a newspaper with very short articles.
- Pinterest: A giant bulletin board to pin ideas and inspiration.

7.5 Top Utility Apps

- A suite of apps from google that replicate apple's functionality, but some user find them more convenient.

  - Google drive
  - Google maps
  - Gmail
  - Google docs
  - Google sheets

- ChatGPT: The most common AI assistant. Much smarter than Siri.

- Calculator: For when you need to crunch some numbers.

7.6 Top Shopping and Food Apps

- Amazon: A giant store with almost anything you can think of.
- eBay: Like a garage sale where you can find both new and used items.
- DoorDash: Food delivery from a variety of restaurants.
- Instacart: For grocery shopping without leaving your home.

7.7 Top Productivity Apps

- Google Calendar: Like a planner for keeping track of appointments.
- Evernote: A more advanced notepad for organizing your thoughts.
- Dropbox: A filing cabinet in the cloud to store your files.
- Zoom: For video calls, like a phone call with video.

Remember, the App Store is a place of discovery and adventure. It's never too lat to learn something new, and your iPad is a wonderful tool to help you do just that

Chapter 8: Exploring Entertainment

Your iPad isn't just a fancy gadget; it's a treasure chest of entertainment! Whether you love reading, gaming, watching movies, or even exercising, your iPad has something for everyone. Let's embark on this journey of digital fun together, step by step.

8.1 How to Read Books and Magazines

Your iPad can be your personal library, brimming with books and magazines.

Using Apple Books:

- Find the 'Books' app (it looks like an open book).
- Browse or search for a book or magazine.
- Tap on the item and then 'Get' or the price to download.
- Once downloaded, tap to open and start reading. Swipe left to turn the pages.

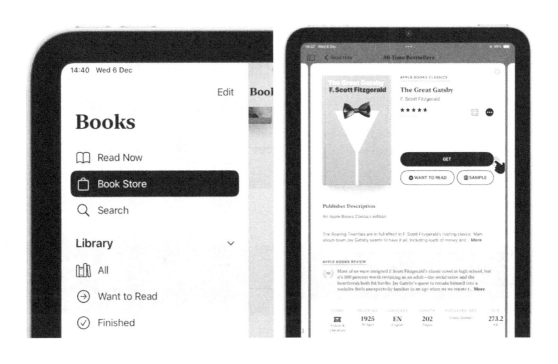

Remember, many classic books are free!

The Apple Books app on your iPad is a versatile tool for reading, much more than just an electronic book. It's like having a customizable book where you can se bookmarks, highlight text, search words, change colors, track your reading progress and even adjust the font size and style to suit your eyes. Let's explore how to make the most of these features:

- Leaving Bookmarks

While reading, tap the upper-right corner of the page. A small bookmark icon wil appear, indicating that you've bookmarked the page. To find your bookmarked pages, tap the table of contents button and select 'Bookmarks'.

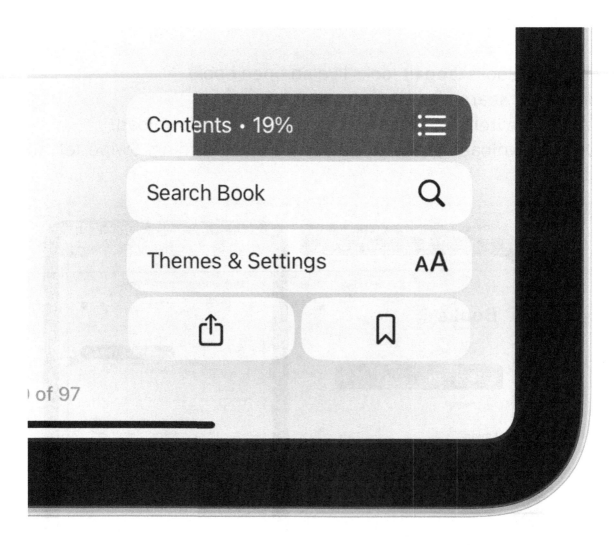

- Highlighting Text

Press and hold a word, then drag the selection handles to highlight. A menu will pop up, where you can choose a color for the highlight. It's like using a highlighter pen in a physical book.

- Searching by Word

Tap the magnifying glass icon at the top. Type in a word or phrase, and the app will show you where it appears in the book. It's like having a search function in your paper book.

- Changing Colors

To change the background color, which can make reading easier on your eyes, tap the 'Aa' icon. You can choose from different color themes like sepia, white, or black (great for night-time reading).

- Saving Your Reading Progress

The app automatically saves your reading progress. When you open the book again, it will start right where you left off. It's like having an automatic bookmark.

- Changing the Font and Size

Tap the 'Aa' icon. Here, you can adjust the font size by sliding the scale. To change the font style, tap 'Font' and choose from the available options. It's like adjusting the lens of your reading glasses.

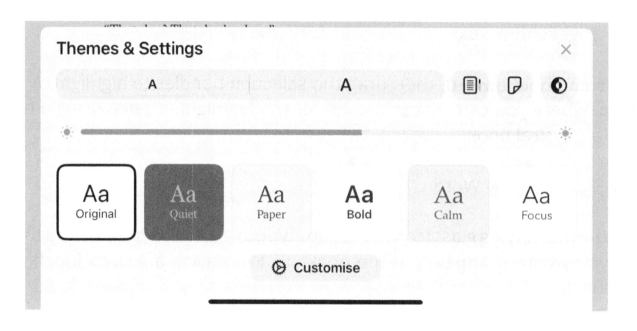

8.2 Playing Games

Games are not just for kids; they're a great way to keep the brain sharp.

Finding Games:

- Open the 'App Store'.
- Tap 'Games' at the bottom.
- Browse or search for a game. Some popular ones for starters include 'Cand Crush' and 'Words With Friends'.
- Tap 'Get' or the price to download.

8.3 Watching Videos and Movies

Your iPad is like a portable cinema.

Using YouTube:

- Find the 'YouTube' app (the red play button).
- Search for a video or select one from the home screen.
- Tap the video to play.

Using Netflix or Other Streaming Apps:

- Download the app from the App Store.
- Open the app and sign in or create an account.
- Browse or search for a movie or show, then tap to play.

8.4 Using Apple TV and Apple Music

Apple TV and Apple Music turn your iPad into a multimedia hub.

Apple TV:

- Open the 'Apple TV' app (the black TV icon).
- Browse or search for a show or movie.
- Select and tap 'Play' or the price to rent/buy.

Apple Music:

- Open 'Music' (the pink-and-white music note).
- Search for an artist, song, or album, or browse the categories.
- Tap a song to play it.

8.5 Take Part in a Workout Class

Keep fit and healthy right from your living room.

Using Fitness Apps:

- Download a fitness app like 'Apple Fitness+' from the App Store.
- Open the app and browse for a workout type you like.
- Select a workout and follow along with the instructor.

Remember, always consult with your doctor before starting any new exercise routine.

Chapter 9: Troubleshooting and Maintenance

Like a beloved car or a cherished garden, your iPad needs a little TLC (Tender Loving Care) to keep running smoothly. In this chapter, we'll cover how to tackle common hiccups, keep your iPad updated, back up your precious data, and maintain your device so it stays as good as new.

9.1 Common Problems and Solutions

1. Your iPad Won't Turn On

- Ensure it's charged adequately. If it doesn't respond, try a force restart: Press and quickly release the Volume Up button, then the Volume Down button. Finally, press and hold the Top button until the Apple logo appears.

2. The Screen Isn't Responding

- Clean the screen gently with a soft, lint-free cloth. If it remains unresponsive, restart your iPad by pressing and holding either the Volume button or the Top button until the slider appears. Drag the slider to turn your device off, then press and hold the Top button until you see the Apple logo.

3. An App Has Become Unresponsive

- Swipe up from the bottom of the screen and pause in the middle to show the app switcher. Then, swipe the unresponsive app's preview upwards to close it. Reopen the app to check if it's working correctly.

4. It Won't Connect to Wi-Fi

- Go to 'Settings' > 'Wi-Fi' and ensure Wi-Fi is enabled. If the problem persist try restarting your router or your iPad. To restart your iPad, follow th method mentioned in the screen responsiveness section.

5. The iPad Isn't Charging

- Inspect the charging cable and USB adapter for any damage. Try a differer power outlet or cable. If it still doesn't charge, try cleaning the charging po carefully with a soft, dry, lint-free cloth.

6. It Runs Slower Than It Used To

- Close apps you're not using by swiping up from the bottom and pausing t open the app switcher, then swipe up on apps to close them. Clearing storag space can also help. Consider deleting unused apps, photos, and videos, c moving them to cloud storage.

7. iPadOS Randomly Crashes

- Update your iPad to the latest version of iPadOS via 'Settings' > 'General' 'Software Update'. If the issue persists and your iPad is functional, tr resetting all settings in 'Settings' > 'General' > 'Reset' > 'Reset All Settings'.

8. You Can't Get Past the Boot Up Screen

- Connect your iPad to a computer and open iTunes (or Finder on macO Catalina or later). Put your iPad in recovery mode: Quickly press and releas the Volume Up button, followed by the Volume Down button. Then, press an hold the Top button until your device begins to restart. Continue holding th Top button until your iPad goes into recovery mode.

9.2 Software Updates

Updating your iPad is like giving it a rejuvenating spa treatment. Here's how to do it:

- Plug your iPad into power and connect to Wi-Fi.
- Go to 'Settings', then 'General', and tap 'Software Update'.
- If an update is available, tap 'Download and Install'.
- After the download, tap 'Install' to update immediately, or choose 'Later' to install it at a more convenient time.
-

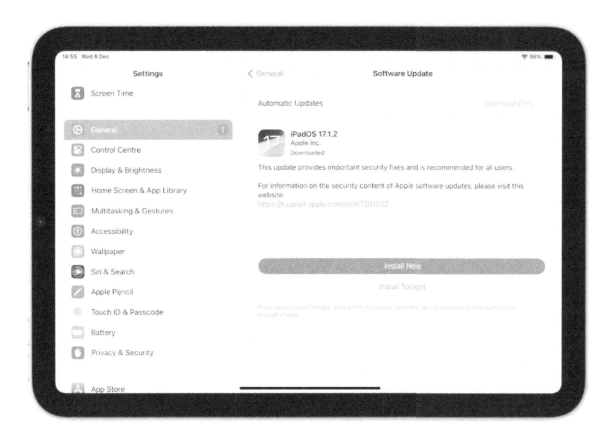

9.3 Backing Up Your iPad

Backing up your iPad is like making a copy of your photo albums for safekeeping. You can use iCloud or your computer for this.

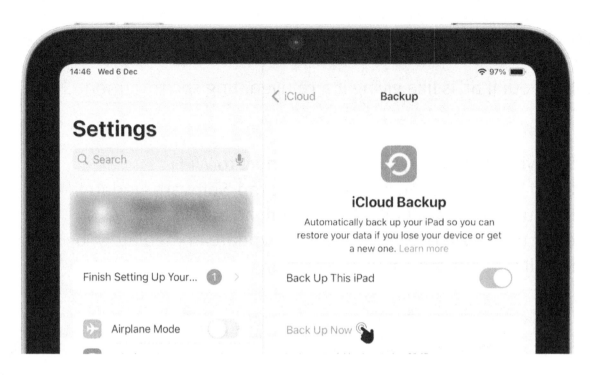

- Using iCloud:

  - Connect to Wi-Fi.
  - Go to 'Settings', tap your name at the top, then tap 'iCloud'.
  - Tap 'iCloud Backup', then 'Back Up Now'.

- Using a Computer:

  - Connect your iPad to your computer.
  - Open iTunes (or Finder if you're on macOS Catalina or later).
  - Select your iPad and click 'Back Up Now'.

9.4 Cleaning and Maintenance Tips

Just like your home needs regular tidying up, your iPad benefits from a bit of digita cleaning and maintenance. Let's look at how you can keep your iPad running smoothly, ensuring it remains fast, efficient, and clutter-free.

Digital Cleaning Tips

- Clear Unused Apps:

  - It's like decluttering your closet. Go through your apps and uninstall those you haven't used in a while. To uninstall an app, press and hold its icon until it jiggles, then tap the 'X' or the '-' icon.

- Manage Storage:

  - Check your iPad's storage in 'Settings' > 'General' > 'iPad Storage'. Here, you can see what's taking up space and decide what to delete, like old videos, photos, or app data.

- Organize Your Home Screen:

  - Like arranging books on a shelf, organize your apps into folders by category. Press and hold an app until it jiggles, then drag it over another app to create a folder.

Clear Safari Cache:

  - Over time, your browser collects data that can slow down your iPad. Clear it by going to 'Settings' > 'Safari' and tap 'Clear History and Website Data'.

iPad Maintenance Tips

- Regularly Restart Your iPad:

  - Just like taking a short nap refreshes you, restarting your iPad can refresh its memory and ensure smoother performance. Hold down the top button and either volume button, then slide to power off.

- Keep iOS Updated:

  - Stay current with the latest iPadOS updates. Go to 'Settings' > 'General' 'Software Update' to check for updates. These updates include performanc improvements and bug fixes.

- Backup Regularly:

  - Regular backups ensure you don't lose important data. Use iCloud or iTune for backup, as discussed earlier in this chapter.

Chapter 10: iCloud

10.1 What is iCloud

Think of iCloud as a magical, invisible storage chest that holds your precious memories and important documents, floating somewhere up in the digital sky. It's a service provided by Apple that keeps your data safe, updated, and available on all your devices. Let's demystify iCloud and learn how to use it effectively.

10.2 Understanding What you Need to Save on iCloud Drive

- Essential Data:
  - Think of iCloud Drive as your personal safety deposit box. Store important documents, photos, and videos. You can also keep your contacts, calendar events, and reminders here.

- App Data:

  - Many apps can save their data to iCloud, ensuring you don't lose your progress in games or important app-specific documents.

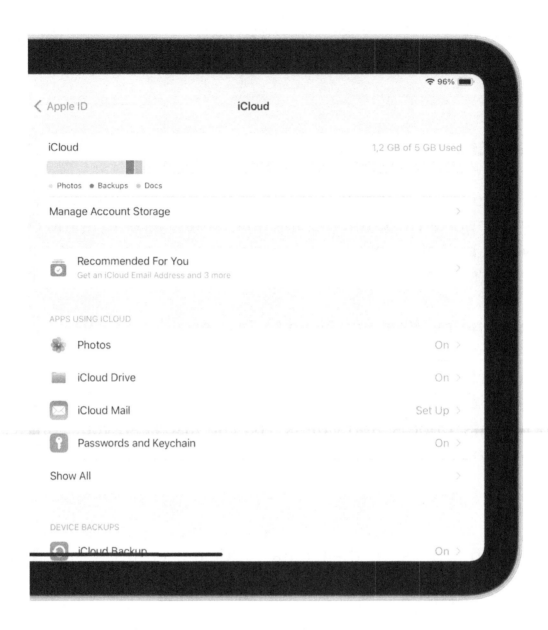

10.3 Tips and Tricks for iCloud

Free Storage:

Apple provides 5 GB of free storage in iCloud, which is like having a small drawer in your digital filing cabinet.

Expanding Storage:

If you need more space, you can buy more storage. Plans range from 50 GB to 2 TB terabytes). Imagine going from a small drawer to a whole wardrobe of space!

Using Free Storage Wisely

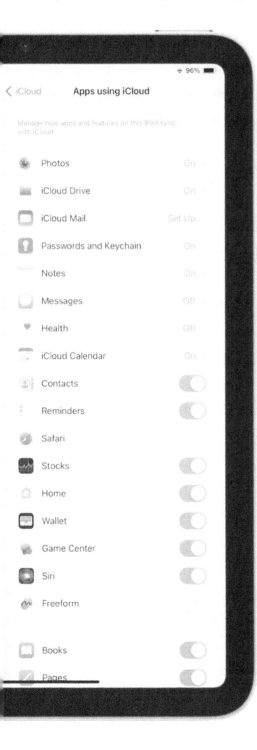

- Prioritize Your Data:

- With 5 GB, you have to be selective. Store essential documents and data.

- Regularly Clean Your iCloud:

- Periodically go through your iCloud Drive and delete files you no longer need, just like tidying up a closet.

Using Paid Storage

- For Heavy Users:

- If you take lots of photos, work with large documents, or use your iPad intensively, paid storage might be necessary.

- Family Sharing:

- You can share a larger iCloud plan with your family. It's like renting a storage unit that the whole family can use.

How to Manage iCloud Storage

- Checking Your Storage:

  - To see how much space you're using, go to 'Settings', tap your name, the 'iCloud'. Here you can see a breakdown of what's using your space.

- Buying More Storage:

  - In the same 'iCloud' section in 'Settings', you can tap 'Manage Storage' 'Change Storage Plan' to upgrade.

Find My iPad:

- Enable 'Find My iPad' in iCloud settings. It's like a GPS tracker for your iPad if ever gets lost.

iCloud Backup:

- Regularly back up your iPad. This is like making a copy of your entire iPad i case you need to restore it later.

Chapter 11: Accessories

Just like a gardener needs a shovel and a painter needs a brush, your iPad can be enhanced with a few key accessories. These tools – the Apple Pencil, Smart Folio, Keyboard, and Mouse – can transform your iPad experience, making it more versatile and enjoyable. Let's explore these wonderful tools.

11.1 Apple pencil

The Apple Pencil is like a magic wand for your iPad. It lets you write, draw, and interact with your iPad in a very natural way.

- Pairing the Apple Pencil:

  - To start using it, simply attach it to the magnetic connector on the side of your iPad (for the 2nd generation Apple Pencil) or plug it into the Lightning port (for the 1st generation). It will pair automatically.

- Using the Apple Pencil:

  - You can write notes, doodle, or navigate your iPad. It's pressure-sensitive, which means the harder you press, the thicker the line in your drawings.

11.2 Smart folio

The Smart Folio is like a cozy coat for your iPad. It protects your device and can also be used as a stand.

- Attaching the Smart Folio:

  - Simply align your iPad with the Folio; it will snap into place magnetically.
  - When you open or close the Folio, your iPad will wake up or go to sleep automatically.

- Using it as a Stand:

  - Fold the Folio to prop up your iPad, perfect for watching videos or making video calls.

11.3 Keyboard

Adding a keyboard to your iPad is like turning it into a mini-computer. It's great for typing emails, documents, or searching the web.

- Connecting a Keyboard:

  - For Apple's Smart Keyboard, just attach it magnetically to your iPad, and you're ready to type.
  - You can also use a Bluetooth keyboard. Turn on Bluetooth in 'Settings', turn on your keyboard, and follow the on-screen instructions to pair it.

11.4 Using a Mouse with iPad

Using a mouse with your iPad might sound unusual, like eating pizza with a fork, but it can be quite handy!

- Pairing a Bluetooth Mouse:

  - Go to 'Settings' > 'Bluetooth', turn on your mouse, and put it in pairing mode. Your iPad will detect the mouse; tap its name to pair.

- Using the Mouse:

  - Once connected, you can use the mouse just like you would on a computer. A cursor will appear on your iPad screen, which you can move around and click on things.

Your iPad is a versatile tool, and with the right accessories, it becomes even more powerful and adaptable. Whether you're an artist, a writer, a casual browser, or a video chat enthusiast, there's an accessory to enhance your experience.

Chapter 12: Productivity

Your iPad is not just a window to the world of entertainment; it's also a powerful tool for productivity. Whether you're taking notes, managing your schedule, or working on documents, your iPad can be as helpful as a Swiss Army knife in your daily life. Let's delve into how you can harness its potential.

12.1 Taking notes

Think of your iPad as your personal notepad, always ready for your thoughts, lists or doodles.

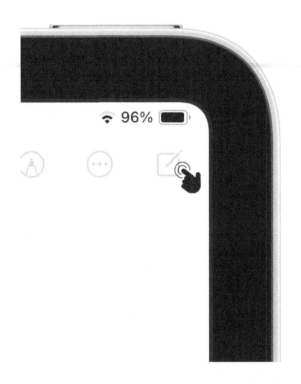

- Using the Notes App:
    - Tap the 'Notes' app.
    - To start a new note, tap the compose button (a square with a pen).
    - Type away! You can also use the Apple Pencil to write or draw.

12.2 Working with Documents

Your iPad can be your portable office, allowing you to create, view, and edit documents on the go.

Using Word Processing Apps:

- Apps like 'Pages' or 'Microsoft Word' can be downloaded from the App Store.
- Open the app and choose to create a new document.
- Use the on-screen keyboard to type, or attach a physical keyboard for more comfort.

Working with PDF Files

- Reading PDFs:

    - To open a PDF, simply tap on it in your email or in the Files app. It will open in a default viewer where you can zoom in or scroll through pages.

- Editing PDFs:

  - For basic edits like highlighting or adding notes, use the Markup tool. While viewing the PDF, tap the Markup icon (a pen tip), then choose a tool to annotate.

- Converting to PDF:

  - You can convert web pages, emails, and documents to PDF. For instance, in Safari, tap the Share icon and select 'Create PDF'.

Adding a Digital Signature

A digital signature on a document is like signing a letter in ink, but it's done electronically.

- Creating a Digital Signature:

  - Open the PDF you need to sign in to the Files app.
  - Tap the Markup icon, then the '+' button.
  - Select 'Signature'. You can then sign using your finger or Apple Pencil.
  - Drag the signature to the right spot in the document.

- Why Use a Digital Signature:

  - It's useful for signing official documents like contracts or forms right from your iPad, without the need to print, sign, and scan.

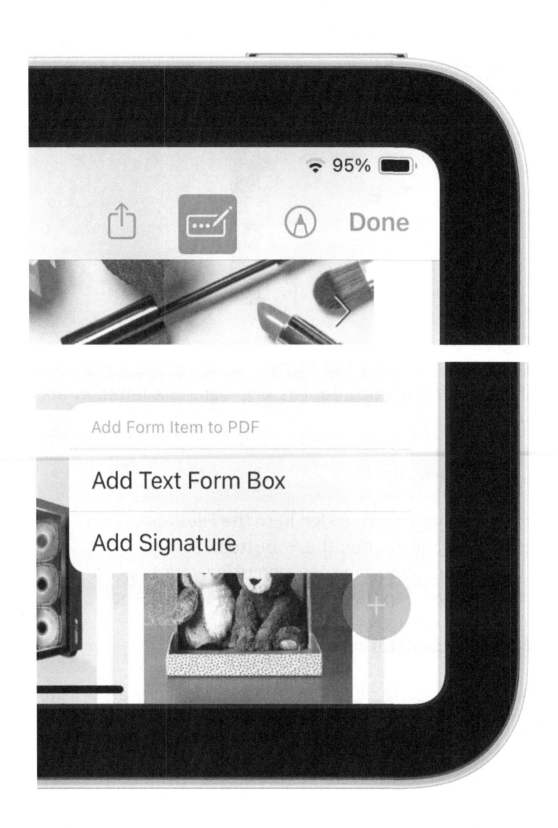

Storing Files in the Files App

The Files app on your iPad works like a filing cabinet, keeping your document organized.

- Using the Files App:

  - Open the 'Files' app.
  - You can see all your documents stored in iCloud Drive or on your iPad.
  - To create a new folder, tap 'Browse' at the bottom, then 'New Folder' in the top-right corner. Name your folder and tap 'Done'.

- Saving Documents to Files:

  - When you create or receive a document, you can save it to the Files app. Tap the Share icon and select 'Save to Files'. Choose the location and tap 'Add'.

12.3 Drawing

Your iPad can transform into an artist's canvas, offering a spectrum of drawing programs suitable for amateurs and professionals. Let's explore how these apps vary and why the Apple Pencil is your best tool for this creative journey.

Drawing Apps: From Amateur to Professional

- For Beginners:

  - Apps like 'Adobe Fresco' and 'Procreate': These apps are user-friendly, making them ideal for beginners. They offer basic drawing tools and simple interfaces. Think of them as your sketchbook and a set of colored pencils – straightforward and fun to use.

- For Intermediate Artists:

  - Apps like 'SketchBook' and 'ArtRage': These offer more advanced tools and features, perfect for those who have some experience with digital art. They're like having a more sophisticated set of art supplies, giving you more control and options.

- For Professionals:

  - Apps like 'Affinity Designer' and 'Adobe Illustrator Draw': These are high-end programs offering precision tools and complex functionalities. They cater to professional artists and designers, akin to a full artist's studio with every tool imaginable.

Why Use the Apple Pencil for Drawing

- Precision and Sensitivity: The Apple Pencil is designed to work seamlessly with your iPad. It offers precision that your finger can't, making it ideal for detailed artwork. It's like the difference between painting with a fine brush versus your finger.

- Pressure Sensitivity: It responds to pressure, allowing you to create lines of varying thickness and opacity, just like a real pencil or brush.

- Tilt Functionality: You can tilt the Apple Pencil to shade an area, much like you would with a graphite pencil.

- Palm Rejection: When using the Apple Pencil, the iPad ignores your palm resting on the screen, ensuring no accidental marks.

Working with Images: Photo Editors

Your iPad can also be a powerful tool for photo editing, turning ordinary photos into stunning visuals.

- For Basic Edits:

  - 'Apple Photos': Built into your iPad, it offers basic editing like cropping, adjusting brightness, and applying filters – perfect for quick, simple edits.

- For More Advanced Edits:

  - 'Adobe Lightroom' and 'Pixelmator': These apps provide more advanced features like retouching, color correction, and layer-based editing. They're like having a digital darkroom at your fingertips.

- For Creative Manipulation:

  - 'Affinity Photo': This is a professional-grade photo editing tool with capabilities akin to Photoshop. It's ideal for creative photo manipulation, complex edits, and graphic design work.

12.4 Managing your Calendar

Your iPad can be your personal assistant, helping you keep track of appointments nd events.

- Using the Calendar App:
  - Open the 'Calendar' app.
  - Tap the '+' sign to add a new event.
  - Fill in the details like date, time, and location.

Consider your iPad's calendar as your personal assistant, helping you keep track of all your appointments, birthdays, anniversaries, and social events. It's like having an always-updated diary at your fingertips. Let's walk through a real-life example relevant to older individuals.

Example: Organizing a Week with the Calendar App

Imagine you're planning your week. You have a doctor's appointment on Tuesday, a coffee date with a friend on Thursday, and your granddaughter's piano recital on Saturday. Here's how you'd manage this using your iPad's Calendar:

- Monday:

  - Morning: Add 'Grocery Shopping at 10 AM'.
  - How to Add: Open the Calendar app, tap the '+' button on the desired date and enter the details..

- Tuesday:

  - Afternoon: Schedule 'Doctor's Appointment at 3 PM'.
  - Setting a Reminder: While adding the event, tap on 'Add Alert' and choose time, like '1 hour before', to get a reminder.

- Wednesday:

  - All Day: It's your friend's birthday.
  - Adding Birthdays: Enter her birthday as an all-day event. You can also set it to repeat annually.

- Thursday:

  - Evening: 'Coffee with John at 6 PM'.
  - Location Reminder: Add the café's location for easy navigation and a reminder when it's time to leave.

- Saturday:

  - Afternoon: 'Emily's Piano Recital at 2 PM'.
  - Invite Family Members: Use the 'Invitees' option to send an invitation to other family members who might want to join.

By the end of this process, your week is neatly organized in your calendar, with reminders set to ensure you don't forget any important events or tasks.

Additional Tips for Calendar Management
  - View Options: Switch between day, week, month, or year views to see your schedule in different formats.

- Customize Alerts: Tailor reminders for different events – some might nee[d] just a 15-minute heads-up, while others, like doctor's appointments, migh[t] need a day-ahead alert.
- Color Coding: Assign different colors to types of events (e.g., medical, socia[l] birthdays) for a quick visual reference.

12.5 To-Do Lists and Reminders

Keep track of your tasks and to-dos effortlessly.

- Using the Reminders App:

  - Open 'Reminders'.
  - Tap 'New Reminder', type in your task, and set a date and time if needed.
  - You can also create different lists for various tasks.
  -

The Difference Between Reminders and Calendar Apps

- Reminders App:

  - Think of the Reminders app as your to-do list. It's designed for tasks that need to be done but don't necessarily have a specific time slot in your day.
  - You can set tasks like "Call the doctor for an appointment" or "Water the plants".
  - Reminders can be set to alert you at a specific time or when you arrive at or leave a location (like reminding you to buy milk when you're near the grocery store).
  - You can organize tasks into lists, prioritize them, and even set recurring reminders for daily activities like taking medication.

- Calendar App:

  - The Calendar app is your scheduling tool. It's ideal for appointments, events, and activities that occur at a specific time and date.
  - You would use the Calendar for things like "Doctor's appointment at 3 PM on Tuesday" or "Lunch with Susan at noon on Friday".
  - It gives you a visual overview of your day, week, month, or year, allowing you to see how your time is allocated.
  - You can also invite others to events and get notified when it's time to leave based on traffic conditions.

- **Example**

  - Monday: Set a reminder to "Check blood pressure" in the morning.
  - Tuesday: Reminder to "Call grandchildren" in the evening.
  - Wednesday: A task to "Water the garden".
  - Thursday: Reminder for "Pick up prescription" when near the pharmacy.
  - Friday: A recurring reminder to "Take weekly medication".

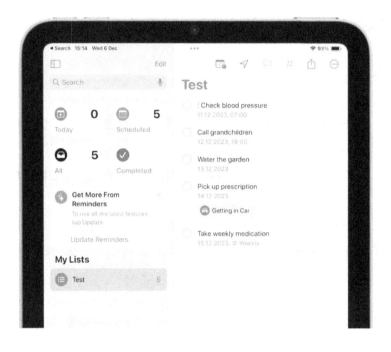

12.6 Focus Mode

Focus mode helps you concentrate b
minimizing distractions.

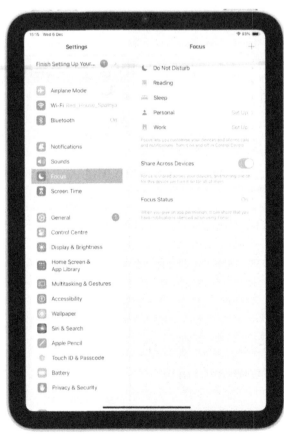

- Setting Up Focus Mode:
    - Go to 'Settings' > 'Focus'.
    - Choose a focus mode like 'Do No
Disturb' or 'Personal'.
    - Customize settings like allowe
notifications and people.

Focus Mode on your iPad is like putting a 'D
Not Disturb' sign on your digital life. It helps yo
concentrate on what's important by minimizin
interruptions from calls, messages, an
notifications. This feature can be especial
helpful for older adults who may want dedicate
time for specific activities without distraction:
Let's explore this with a real-life example.

Example: Using Focus Mode for Reading Time

Imagine you have set aside the afternoon for some quiet reading - perhaps the latest mystery novel or poetry collection. However, constant notifications can be quite distracting. Here's how you can use Focus Mode:

- Setting Up Reading Focus:

  - Go to 'Settings' > 'Focus'.
  - Tap 'Do Not Disturb' or create a new Focus by tapping the '+' in the top-right corner and naming it 'Reading'.
  - Customize it by selecting allowed notifications (if any). For instance, you might want to allow calls from close family members for emergencies.

- Activating Reading Focus:

  - Swipe down from the top-right corner of your iPad to access the Control Center.
  - Tap the Focus button (crescent moon icon) and select your 'Reading' Focus.
  - Now, app notifications and contacts not in your allowed list will be silenced.

- Scheduling Focus Time:

  - You can schedule this Focus mode to automatically activate during your usual reading hours. For instance, every day from 2 PM to 4 PM.

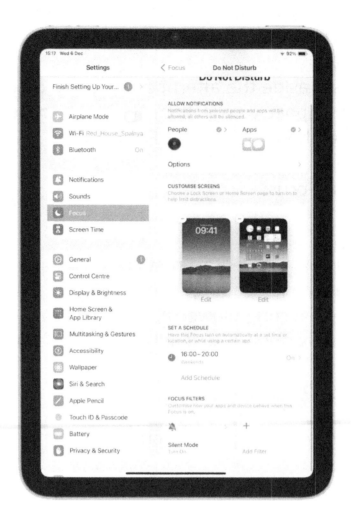

Benefits for Older Adults

- Minimizing Distractions: Focus Mode helps create a peaceful environment, allowing you to immerse yourself in your reading without interruptions.
- Maintaining Routine: By scheduling Focus times, you can establish and maintain a daily routine, which can be both comforting and beneficial for overall well-being.
- Emergency Accessibility: You can still allow important contacts (like family members) to reach you, ensuring peace of mind.

12.7 Multitasking on Ipad

Your iPad allows you to work on two apps at the same time, like having two books open on a desk.

- Using Split View:

    - Open an app.
    - Swipe up slightly from the bottom to bring up the Dock.
    - Drag another app from the Dock to the left or right edge of the screen.

Example: Researching a Recipe While Writing a Shopping List

Suppose you want to bake a special cake for your grandchild's birthday. You need to find a recipe and simultaneously write down the ingredients you'll need to buy. Here's how you can use multitasking on your iPad:

- Opening the Recipe App and Notes Side by Side:

    - First, open the app where you want to find a cake recipe, such as Safari.
    - Swipe up slightly from the bottom to bring up the Dock without closing Safari.
    - On the Dock, find and drag the 'Notes' app to the right or left edge of the screen. This opens Notes in a smaller window beside Safari.

- Using Slide Over:

  - Alternatively, you can use Slide Over for a more temporary multitaskin
    experience. Drag the 'Notes' app to the center of the screen, and it hover
    over Safari in a smaller window.

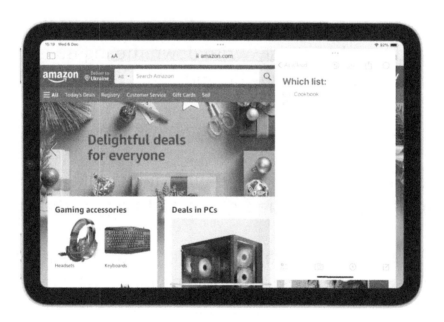

- Adjusting the Screens:

  - You can adjust the size of both apps by dragging the bar that divides them. This way, you can see both the recipe and your notes at a size that's comfortable for you.

- Taking Notes While Viewing the Recipe:

  - As you find the ingredients in the recipe, you can easily switch to the Notes app to write them down, all without having to switch back and forth between full-screen apps.

12.8 Printing From your iPad

Print documents or photos directly from your iPad, as easily as sending a letter.

- Using AirPrint:

  - Ensure your printer supports AirPrint and is connected to the same Wi-Fi network as your iPad.
  - In the app, tap the share button (a square with an arrow) and choose 'Print'.
  - Select your printer and tap 'Print'.

Chapter 13: Shortcuts and Automatisation

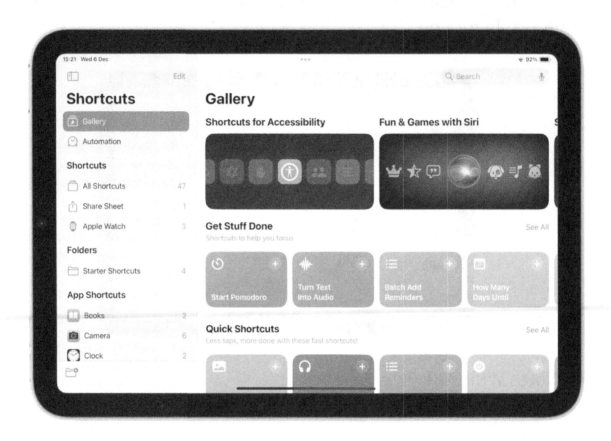

13.1 Basics of iPad Shortcuts

Imagine having a magic wand that can perform small tasks for you with a single tap. That's what shortcuts on your iPad are like! They can automate routine tasks making your iPad experience smoother and more enjoyable.

● How to Access Shortcuts:

• You'll find the 'Shortcuts' app on your iPad. It's where you can create and manage your shortcuts.

- Creating a Basic Shortcut:

  - Open the 'Shortcuts' app and tap the '+' icon to create a new shortcut.
  - You can choose from a list of actions, like sending a message or playing music.

13.2 What it can do

Think of shortcuts as your personal assistants, capable of doing a variety of tasks:

- Send Automated Messages: Like reminding your family member about dinner every Thursday.
- Open Your Daily News: With a single tap, open your favorite news site every morning.
- Set Reminders for Regular Tasks: Like watering the plants or taking medications.

13.3 Best Shortcuts That You Really Need

Exploring shortcuts on your iPad doesn't require you to be a tech wizard. The Shortcuts app comes with a gallery of ready-made shortcuts, a bit like a cookbook full of recipes that you can use without having to mix the ingredients yourself. Here are some particularly useful ones:

- Convert Text to Audio:

  - Perfect for turning written articles or emails into spoken words, ideal for listening while you're engaged in other activities, like knitting or gardening.

- Laundry Timer:

  - Set a timer for your laundry, so you don't have to keep checking if it's done. It's like having a little reminder that nudges you when it's time to switch the laundry.

- Translate Text:

  - Quickly translate text into another language. It's handy when you're trying to understand a recipe in a foreign language or communicate with someone who speaks a different language.

- Read Later:

  - Save interesting articles or websites to read at your convenience. It's like bookmarking pages in a book for later enjoyment.

- Word of the Day:

  - Expand your vocabulary with a new word every day. It's a fun and educational way to keep your mind sharp.

Example: Using the 'Laundry Timer' Shortcut

Let's walk through a practical example of using the 'Laundry Timer' shortcut tailored for older adults. Imagine you have just put a load of laundry in the washer and now you want to relax with a book or a cup of tea without worrying about keeping track of time. Here's how the 'Laundry Timer' shortcut can help:

- Setting Up the 'Laundry Timer' Shortcut:

- Find the Shortcut:

- Open the 'Shortcuts' app on your iPad.
- Go to the 'Gallery' tab at the bottom.
- Search for 'Laundry Timer' in the search bar or browse through the list to find it.

- Add the Shortcut:

  - Tap on 'Laundry Timer'.
  - Review what the shortcut does and tap 'Add Shortcut' to add it to your collection.

- Use the Shortcut:

  - Return to the 'My Shortcuts' tab.
  - Find and tap on the 'Laundry Timer' shortcut.
  - When prompted, enter the number of minutes your laundry will take (e.g., 45 minutes).

- Relax and Wait:

  - Now that the timer is set, you can go about your other activities. The shortcut will alert you when your laundry is done.

13.4 Adding Shortcuts to Your Home Screen

Once you find shortcuts that make your life easier, you can add them to your iPad's home screen, just like placing your most-used tools on a workbench for easy access. This way, these shortcuts are just a tap away, ready to assist you whenever you need them.

- Edit the Shortcut:

  - Tap on the 'Laundry Timer' shortcut in the 'Shortcuts' app.

- Tap on the three dots (...) in the upper-right corner of the shortcut.

- Add to Home Screen:

  - Tap 'Add to Home Screen'.
  - Follow the instructions to create an icon for this shortcut on your home screen.

- Use it Directly from the Home Screen:

  - Next time you do laundry, simply tap this new icon on your home screen to set the timer.

Chapter 14: Working with Siri

Imagine having a personal assistant who's always ready to help, day or night. That's Siri on your iPad! Siri can perform tasks, answer questions, and even have a chat with you. Let's discover what Siri can do and how to make the most of this helpful feature.

14.1 What Siri can Do for You

Before diving in, make sure Siri is set up:

- Enable Siri:

  - Go to 'Settings' > 'Siri & Search'.
  - Turn on 'Listen for "Hey Siri"' to activate Siri with your voice, or 'Press Side Button for Siri' to activate with a button press.

- Customize Siri:

  - In the same settings, you can choose Siri's voice and language to suit your preference.

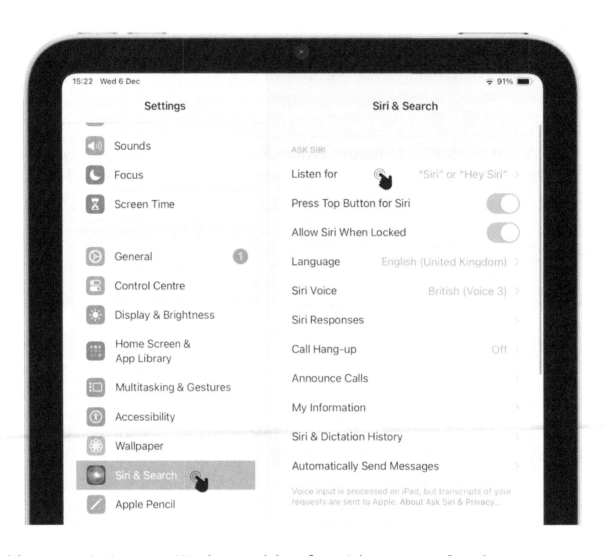

Siri is like a genie in your iPad, capable of a wide range of tasks:

- Make Calls and Send Messages: Just ask Siri to call a friend or send message.
- Set Reminders and Alarms: Siri can remind you of appointments or wake yo up in the morning.
- Provide Information: Whether it's the weather forecast or the latest news, Si has the answers.
- Play Music or Podcasts: Tell Siri what you'd like to listen to.
- Navigate and Give Directions: Ask for directions to a location, and Siri w guide you.

14.2 How to Make Siri Smarter. Chatgpt Integration

The more you use Siri, the better it gets at understanding your preferences and speech patterns.

- Be Specific: When you ask Siri for something, be as specific as possible.
- Correct Siri Politely: If Siri misunderstands, you can correct it by saying, "I meant..." or "No, Siri, try..."
- Use Siri Regularly: The more you interact with Siri, the more it learns about your language and preferences.

ChatGPT integration

Imagine giving Siri, your iPad's helpful assistant, an extra intelligence boost. That's exactly what integrating ChatGPT with Siri does! It's like equipping your friendly assistant with a vast encyclopedia. Let's walk through this process, making it simple and understandable.

1. Downloading the SiriGPT Shortcut

- Finding the Shortcut

    - Think of a shortcut as a recipe. You need to first get the recipe before you can use it. Open your Safari app and visit the SiriGPT shortcut page.

- Look for the button that says 'Add Shortcut' and tap it. It's like adding a new recipe to your cookbook.

2. Gathering Your OpenAI API Keys

- Accessing OpenAI

  - Visit platform.openai.com on your iPad. This is like going to a specific store to get a special ingredient for your recipe.
  - Log in to your account. If you don't have one, you'll need to create it.
  - Tap the three lines in the top right corner, then find your profile at the bottom of the menu.
  - Here, you'll find an option to view your API keys – these are like special codes that let Siri talk to ChatGPT.

3. Copying Your Secret API Key

- Creating and Copying the Key:

  - Select 'Create new secret key'. This key is a unique code – treat it like a secret password.
  - Tap the copy icon to copy this key, then close the window.

4. Adding Your API Key to the SiriGPT Shortcut

- Editing the Shortcut
  - Now, open the 'Shortcuts' app on your iPad.
  - Find the SiriGPT shortcut you just added and tap the three dots to edit it.
  - Paste your API key where it says "ADD API KEY HERE".

5. Enabling Dictation

● Setting Up Dictation

  ● Within the shortcut, scroll down until you see 'Enable Dictation' under a red warning flag.
  ● If you don't see this, you might already have Dictation enabled, and you can skip to the next step.
  ● If it's there, tap it and turn on Dictation. This allows you to speak to Siri instead of typing.

6. Allowing Speech Recognition Access

● Granting Permission

  ● Back in the Shortcuts menu, tap on SiriGPT.
  ● A message will pop up asking for permission to access Speech Recognition. This lets you talk to ChatGPT through Siri. Tap 'Allow'.

7. Allowing SiriGPT to Use Your OpenAI API

● Final Permissions

  ● Run the SiriGPT shortcut by tapping it.
  ● A message will ask for permission to send text to the OpenAI API – this is what allows Siri to understand and answer your questions using ChatGPT. Choose 'Always Allow' or 'Allow Once'.

8. Finishing the Interaction

● Using SiriGPT

- After asking a question and getting an answer from SiriGPT, you can ta
  'Done'.
- If you have more questions, tap 'Ask Again', then 'Done' when finished.
- You can access this enhanced Siri through the Shortcuts app wheneve
  needed.

14.3 Best Prompts for Siri

Here are some useful prompts you can use with Siri:

Siri Command	Description
"What time is it?"	Siri will tell you the current time. Great for when you can't see a clock.
"Tell me about today's weather."	Get a quick overview of the day's weather conditions.
"Is it raining?"	Check if you need an umbrella before heading out.
"How is traffic today?"	Find out traffic conditions, especially useful before a commute.
"What is the etymology of [word]?"	Learn the origin of a specific word. A treat for language enthusiasts.
"How much is gas right now?"	Get current gas prices, helpful for planning trips or errands.
"Tell me a synonym for [word]."	Expand your vocabulary by finding synonyms.

"What is the definition of [word]?"	Quickly look up the meaning of a word.
"When is [holiday]?"	Find out the date of a specific holiday.
"Is [business name] open right now?"	Check if a local store or restaurant is currently open.
"What time is it in [location]?"	Useful for checking the time in different time zones.
"Show me [food type] recipes."	Get culinary inspiration for your next meal.
"How do I make [drink/food name]?"	Step-by-step guidance for preparing a specific dish or drink.
"How many calories are in [food/drink name]?"	Keep track of your dietary intake with calorie information.
"Set a timer for [time duration]."	Handy for cooking, exercising, or any timed activity.
"Wake me up at [time]."	Set an alarm for a specific time.
"Set an appointment with [name] at [time]."	Schedule your appointments effortlessly.
"Cancel appointment with [name] at [time]."	Easily cancel scheduled appointments.
"Remind me to [reminder] at [time, date, location]."	Set reminders for tasks at a particular time, date, or place.

Conclusion

As we close this book, 'iPad for Seniors & Beginners,' think of it not as the end, but as the beginning of an exciting journey with your iPad. You've learned how to navigate its features, from browsing the internet and managing your calendar to using Siri and exploring shortcuts. Each chapter was a step towards becoming more comfortable and confident in using this remarkable device.

Remember, learning new technology, much like gardening or cooking, is a process that flourishes with patience and practice. Don't be discouraged by small hiccups along the way; they are stepping stones to mastery.

Your iPad is a portal to the world, a window to endless information, entertainment and connection. It's a tool that can simplify tasks, bring you closer to loved ones, and open up new horizons of knowledge and fun.

"Age is no barrier when it comes to the heart of learning."

Whether it's keeping in touch with family, enjoying your favorite books and music or exploring new hobbies, your iPad is your companion through it all. Embrace this journey, stay curious, and let your iPad be a source of joy, learning, and discovery in your golden years.

Happy exploring!

Made in the USA
Las Vegas, NV
15 April 2024

88731811R00066